Animal Man

VOLUME 3 ROTWORLD - THE RED KINGDOM

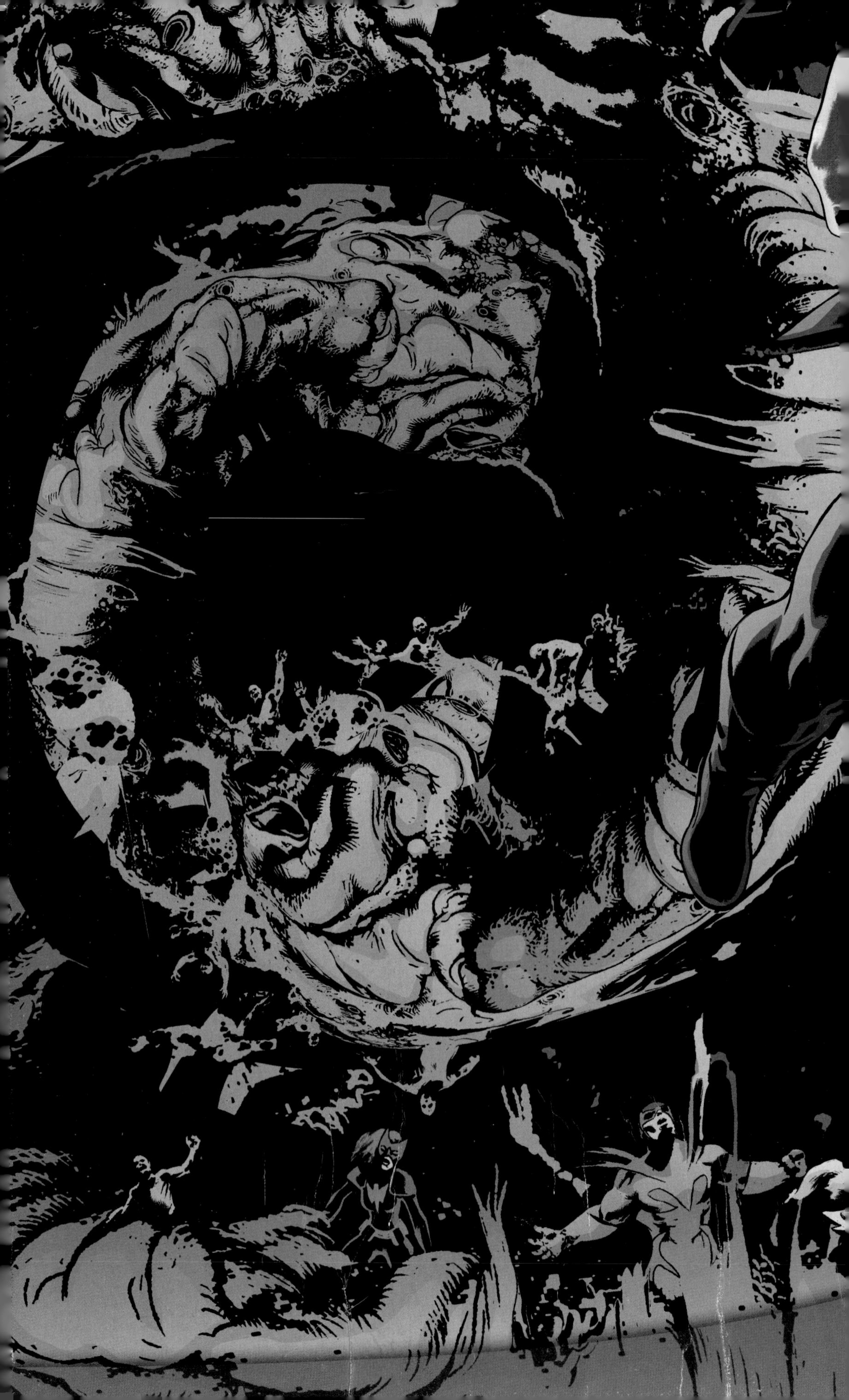

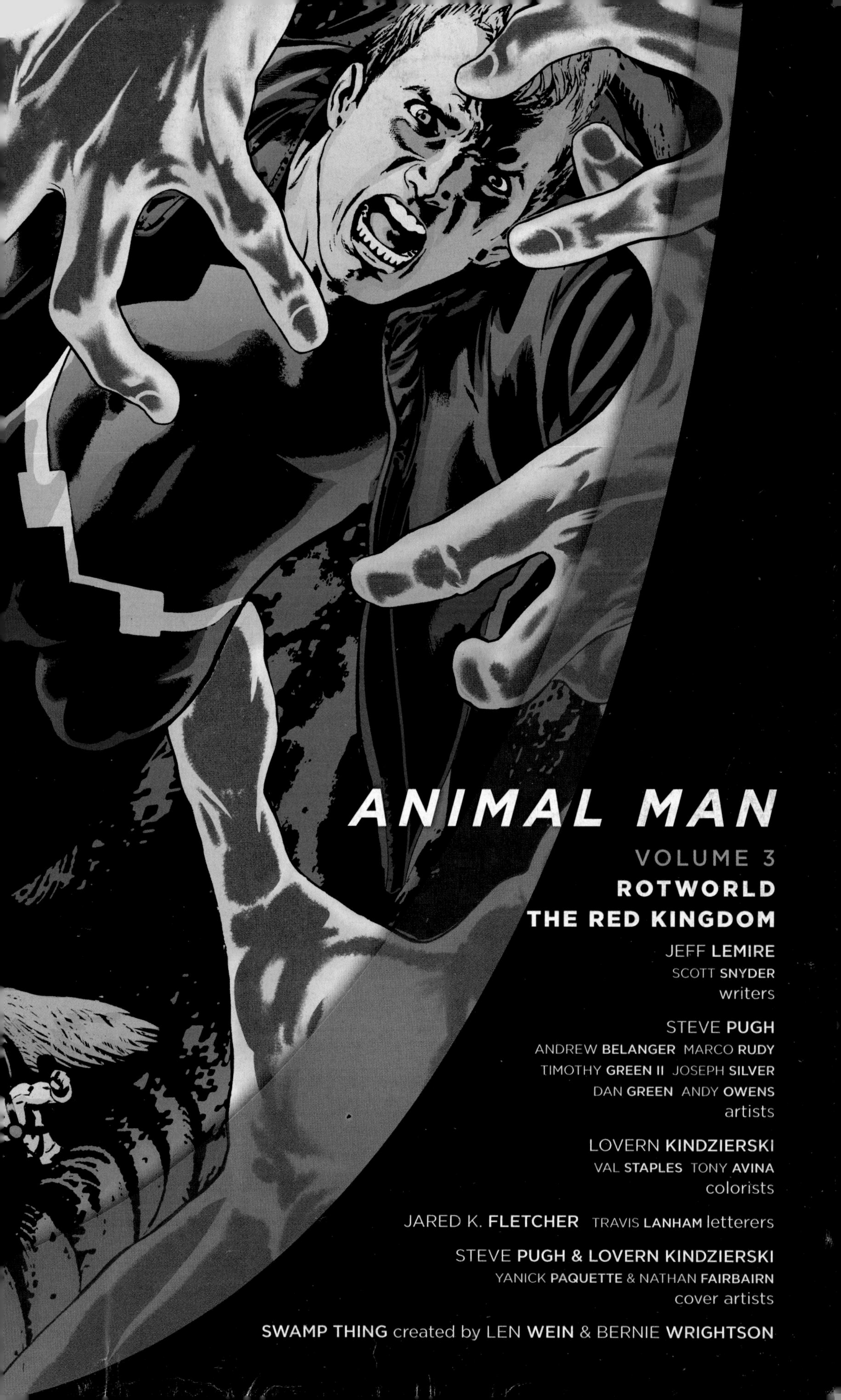

ANIMAL MAN

VOLUME 3
ROTWORLD
THE RED KINGDOM

JEFF **LEMIRE**
SCOTT **SNYDER**
writers

STEVE **PUGH**
ANDREW **BELANGER** MARCO **RUDY**
TIMOTHY **GREEN II** JOSEPH **SILVER**
DAN **GREEN** ANDY **OWENS**
artists

LOVERN **KINDZIERSKI**
VAL **STAPLES** TONY **AVINA**
colorists

JARED K. **FLETCHER** TRAVIS **LANHAM** letterers

STEVE **PUGH & LOVERN KINDZIERSKI**
YANICK **PAQUETTE** & NATHAN **FAIRBAIRN**
cover artists

SWAMP THING created by LEN **WEIN** & BERNIE **WRIGHTSON**

ANIMAL MAN VOLUME 3: ROTWORLD - THE RED KINGDOM

DC Comics, 1700 Broadway, New York, NY 10019
A Warner Bros. Entertainment Company.
Printed by RR Donnelley, Salem, VA, USA. 8/2/13. First Printing.
ISBN: 978-1-4012-4262-6

Library of Congress Cataloging-in-Publication Data

Lemire, Jeff.
Animal Man. Volume 3, Rotworld: The Red Kingdom / Jeff Lemire, Steve Pugh.
pages cm
"Originally published in single magazine form in Animal Man 12-19, Swamp Thing 12, 17."
ISBN 978-1-4012-4262-6
1. Graphic novels. I. Pugh, Steve. II. Title. III. Title: Rotworld. IV. Title: Red kingdom.
PN6728.A58L48 2013
741.5'973-dc23
2013016904

Certified Chain of Custody
At Least 20% Certified Forest Content
www.sfiprogram.org
SFI-01042
APPLIES TO TEXT STOCK ONLY

Since the dawn of time, the fate of the universe has depended on the balance between three forces: THE RED, THE GREEN and THE ROT.

The Red connects all living animals; The Green, all plant life. Both fight to maintain power over the forces of death and decay.

Every generation, The Red selects an avatar as a protector, and its newest is four-year-old Maxine Baker, daughter of Buddy Baker, the super hero called ANIMAL MAN.

But the moment Maxine revealed her powers, agents of The Rot were dispatched to destroy her. Forced from their home, the Baker family went on the run, aided only by their guide "Socks," a house cat and former avatar of The Red.

Knowing that their family's best shot at survival is to join forces with The Rot's other great enemy, the Bakers have been traveling in search of the avatar of The Green, the SWAMP THING.

But The Rot was never far behind them, and now it has taken hold of the Bakers' son Cliff...

JEFF LEMIRE & SCOTT SNYDER
writers

STEVE PUGH
artist

STEVE PUGH & YANICK PAQUETTE
cover artists

LOUISIANA.
SWAMP WATER INN
"THIS IS MY FAULT.
THIS IS ALL MY FAULT. I'M YOUR MOTHER. I'M SUPPOSED TO PROTECT YOU. I'M SUPPOSED TO KEEP YOU SAFE.
BUT I DIDN'T. I LET HIM HAVE HIS WAY, LIKE ALWAYS, AND HERE YOU ARE..."
...MY BABY.
ELLEN... IT'S TIME TO GO.
I--OKAY... I'LL BE RIGHT THERE.

ARE YOU SURE YOU WANT TO COME? WE'LL BE FINE. MAYBE YOU SHOULD STAY WITH CLIFF AND YOUR MOM?
NO! THERE IS NO WAY I'M LETTING YOU TAKE MAXINE OUT THERE WITHOUT ME. SHE NEEDS ME.
MY LITTLE GIRL NEEDS ME!
I STILL DON'T UNDERSTAND WHY WE AREN'T TAKING CLIFFORD TO A HOSPITAL?! THIS IS INSANE!
I TOLD YOU, MARY, THIS THING THAT HURT CLIFF... THAT MONSTER... THERE IS NO DOCTOR THAT CAN HELP THAT.
PLUS I'M STILL WANTED FOR QUESTIONING IN DETECTIVE KRENSHAW'S DEATH. I REALLY THINK OUR BEST CHANCE TO HELP HIM IS OUT THERE...IN THE SWAMP.

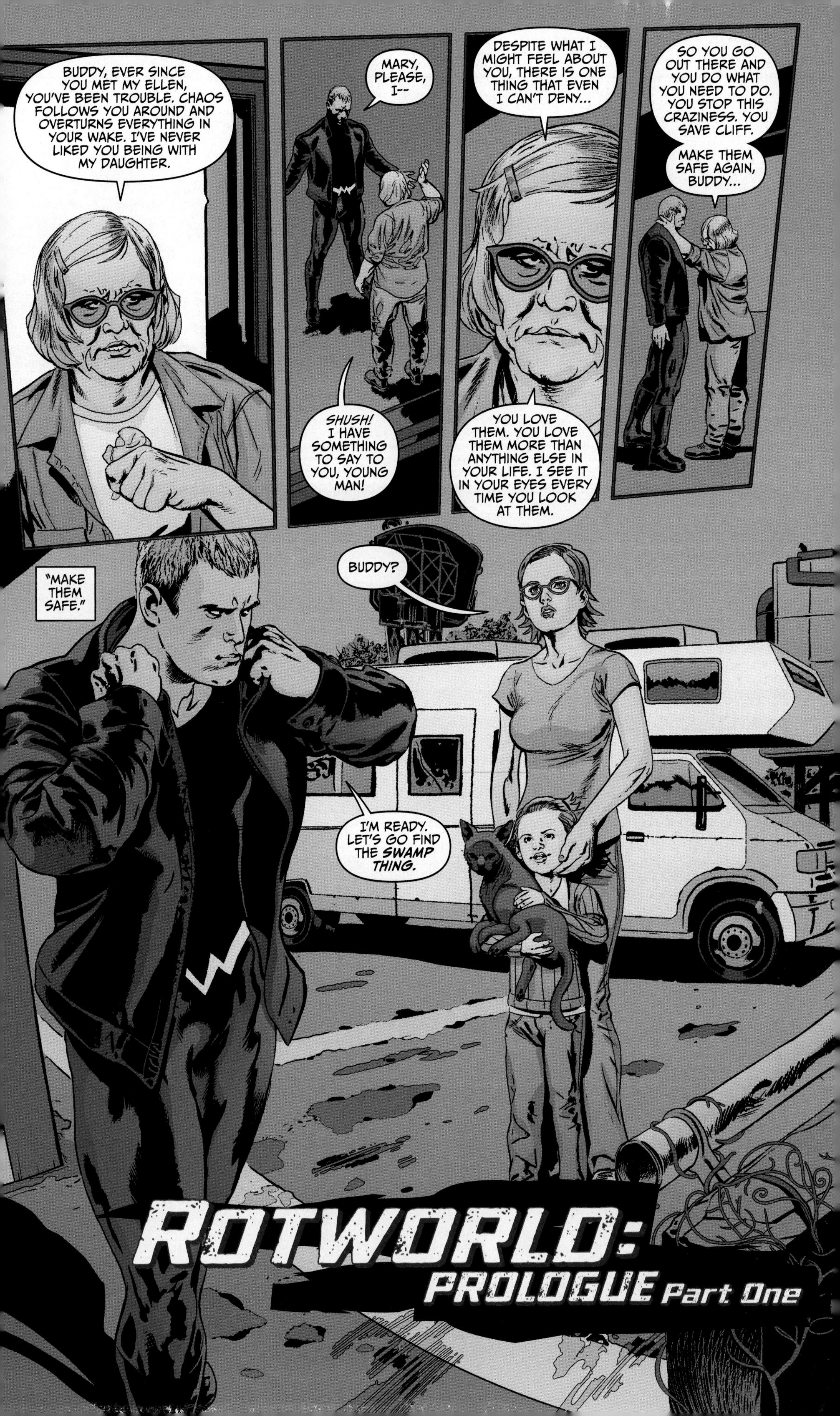
BUDDY, EVER SINCE YOU MET MY ELLEN, YOU'VE BEEN TROUBLE. CHAOS FOLLOWS YOU AROUND AND OVERTURNS EVERYTHING IN YOUR WAKE. I'VE NEVER LIKED YOU BEING WITH MY DAUGHTER.
MARY, PLEASE, I--
SHUSH! I HAVE SOMETHING TO SAY TO YOU, YOUNG MAN!
DESPITE WHAT I MIGHT FEEL ABOUT YOU, THERE IS ONE THING THAT EVEN I CAN'T DENY...
YOU LOVE THEM. YOU LOVE THEM MORE THAN ANYTHING ELSE IN YOUR LIFE. I SEE IT IN YOUR EYES EVERY TIME YOU LOOK AT THEM.
SO YOU GO OUT THERE AND YOU DO WHAT YOU NEED TO DO. YOU STOP THIS CRAZINESS. YOU SAVE CLIFF.
MAKE THEM SAFE AGAIN, BUDDY...
"MAKE THEM SAFE."
BUDDY?
I'M READY. LET'S GO FIND THE SWAMP THING.
ROTWORLD:
PROLOGUE Part One

ARE WE THERE YET, DADDY? I WANNA SEE THE SWAMP MAN!
I WISH I KNEW, LITTLE WING. TRUTH IS, I DON'T EVEN REALLY KNOW WHERE TO START LOOKING.
WELL, THEN, YOU'RE LUCKY I'M HERE, BUDDY BAKER. I CAN SENSE ALEC HOLLAND'S POWER ALL AROUND THIS PLACE. WE ARE CLOSE.
AND HOW CAN YOU "SENSE" THIS ALEC HOLLAND IF HE'S NOT EVEN A PART OF THE RED?
THE RED AND THE GREEN ARE CONNECTED, BUDDY. AS IS THE ROT. TO IMMERSE YOURSELF IN ONE IS TO IMMERSE YOURSELF IN ALL THREE.
LET'S JUST HURRY UP. IT'S GOING TO BE DARK SOON, AND IF THIS GUY CAN HELP CLIFF, I WANT TO GET HIM BACK TO THE HOTEL AS SOON AS POSSIBLE.
YOU MISUNDERSTAND, ELLEN BAKER... ALEC HOLLAND IS NO HEALER.
TO SAVE CLIFF... TO SAVE US ALL, BUDDY AND HOLLAND WILL NEED TO JOIN THEIR POWER. BECOME THE WARRIOR KINGS THEY WERE CREATED TO BE AND ERADICATE THE THREAT AT ITS SOURCE.
SNIFF SNIFF
GREAT, I'M TIRED OF RUNNING. I STILL CAN'T-- I DON'T KNOW, FEEL HIM?
DIG DEEPER, BUDDY BAKER. LET YOUR CONSCIOUSNESS TOUCH THE NEAR INFINITE NUMBER OF LIVING THINGS THAT SWARM THIS OLD SWAMP...

ECOME ONE WITH THE
ED, THE REALM THAT
ONNECTS ALL FAUNA...
"FEEL THE POWERFUL ALLIGATOR THAT HUNTS THESE MUDDY WATERS.
"THAT ALLIGATOR FEEDS ON A THRUSH. TAKES IT IN. THEY BECOME ONE.
"THAT LITTLE THRUSH HAD JUST EATEN ONE OF THE PLANTS FROM THE RIVERBED. CAN YOU FEEL IT DIGESTING IN ITS GULLET?"
"Y-YES..."
"IT IS HERE THAT YOU CAN TOUCH THE MIND OF THE SWAMP THING...DO YOU SENSE HIM, BUDDY BAKER?"
"THE GREEN WAS IN THAT LITTLE BIRD'S BLOODSTREAM...AND NOW IT IS IN THE CROC...AND FROM THE CROC...TO YOU...

YES! I-I SAW HIM...I FELT HIM IN MY MIND!
THIS WAY!
BUDDY!?
I FEEL HIM TOO, DADDY! HE'S SO COLD AND GREEN! LIKE A SALAD! BUT I SENSE A BAD THING WITH HIM...
IT IS A RIFT BETWEEN TWO WORLDS--BE CAREFUL!
MAXINE! WAIT!
MAXINE, WAIT FOR--
OH MY GOD!

COME WITH ME. WE SHOULD GET AWAY FROM IT.
NO, ALEC... WE NEED TO ENTER IT. ANIMAL MAN AND SWAMP THING TOGETHER. NOW.
YOU'RE BUDDY BAKER? I FELT YOU IN THE GREEN.
YES. WE'VE COME A LONG WAY TO FIND YOU.
WE--WE NEED YOUR HELP.

UNNNGHHH
CLIFFORD?!
CLIFF, SWEETHEART, CAN YOU HEAR ME?
SSSSSS...
DEAR LORD, YOU'RE BURNING UP!
LET ME GET YOU A COLD CLOTH... I'LL BE RIGHT BACK, DEAR.
...OH, I HOPE YOUR MOTHER AND FATHER GET BACK SOON... I DON'T LIKE THIS AT ALL.
WE SHOULD GET YOU TO A REAL DOCT--?
CLIFFORD?
CLIFF!?

I'D LOVE TO TELL YOU HOW WE ENDED UP HERE, BUT THE STORY IS TOTALLY INSANE. I DOUBT YOU'D BELIEVE ME.
OH, YOU'D BE SURPRISED.
I'M *ABBY,* BY THE WAY.
ALEC AND I HAVEN'T EXACTLY HAD THE MOST NORMAL OF LIVES LATELY.
I THINK YOU SHOULD START AT THE BEGINNING... IT MIGHT HELP US UNDERSTAND WHY YOU THINK WE'RE SUPPOSED TO HELP EACH OTHER.
IT SEEMS LIKE MONTHS SINCE WE'VE BEEN ON THE RUN. IT'S ALMOST HARD TO REMEMBER WHEN IT STARTED. BUT I GUESS IT WAS WITH YOU, MAXINE...WITH THE PETS.
YEAH...I GOT ANIMAL POWERS LIKE MY DAD.
"SO WE WENT ON AN ADVENTURE TO THE RED PLACE...AND WE MET THE TOTEMS...ALL THE OLD ANIMAL MEN AND WOMEN LIKE ME AND MY DAD.
"THEY TOLD ME I WAS THE NEW...WHAT WAS IT CALLED, DADDY? AVIATOR OF THE RED?"
AVATAR, LITTLE WING. YOU'RE THE NEW *AVATAR* OF THE RED.
AND YOU... ALEC, YOU'RE THE AVATAR OF THE GREEN?
YES. IT'S TAKEN ME A WHILE TO ACCEPT MY PLACE... BUT I AM.

RIGHT. WELL, AROUND THIS TIME, THE ROT SENT THESE CREEPY BASTARDS CALLED THE *HUNTERS THREE* AFTER US. MAXINE AND I TOOK OUT TWO OF THEM IN THE RED, BUT ONE WENT AFTER ELLEN AND CLIFF IN OUR HOME.
"I WENT BACK TO SAVE THEM AND FINALLY MANAGED TO BEAT THE DAMN THING. OR SO I THOUGHT...
"THEN IT POSSESSED MY BODY, BUT I GREW A NEW ONE. AND I FINALLY KILLED IT.
"BUT IT JUST INFECTED... OR *POSSESSED* ALL THE ANIMALS IN THE AREA AND WE HAD TO GO ON THE RUN, *AGAIN*...THAT'S WHEN WE CAME LOOKING FOR YOU.
"BUT MY SON, CLIFF, WAS HURT. I DON'T KNOW WHAT'S WRONG WITH HIM...WHAT *THAT THING* DID TO HIM."

IT SEEMS OUR PATHS HAVE BEEN ENTWINED. WE HAVE BEEN STRUGGLING AGAINST THE SAME THING...OR AT LEAST SOME VARIATION OF IT...*THE ROT.*
WELL, MY LITTLE BOY IS SICK. AND UNLESS WE DO SOMETHING, THE ROT IS JUST GOING TO KEEP COMING AND COMING. WE NEED TO GO IN THERE AND STOP IT!
BUDDY! WHAT ARE YOU TALKING ABOUT? WE'RE HERE TO HELP CLIFF, NOT RUN OFF ON SOME NEW FIGHT!
ELLEN, DON'T YOU UNDERSTAND?!
THIS ISN'T ABOUT RUNNING AWAY. THIS IS ABOUT FACING THIS THING HEAD ON, ONCE AND FOR ALL! MAYBE THE ONLY WAY TO REALLY HELP CLIFF IS TO WIPE THESE DAMN MONSTERS OUT OF EXISTENCE!
MOMMY... DADDY... STOP FIGHTING. LOOK!
MAXINE... GET AWAY FROM THERE!
O, MOMMY, OK! IT'S ME! UT WHY IS VERYTHING BURNING? ID--DID I DO THAT?

"IT'S...IT'S A TERRIBLE PLACE, MOMMY...FULL OF DEAD THINGS.
"BUT THERE'S STILL SOME GOOD THERE, TOO. I CAN SEE IT.
"BUT NOT FOR LONG. THE DEAD THINGS ARE COMING...GETTING BIGGER AND BIGGER.
"AND WHO IS THAT SCARY MAN, MOMMY? I FEEL LIKE I KNOW HIM...LIKE I'VE SEEN HIM BEFORE?"

HONEY, ON'T SEE NYTHING. ASE COME AY FROM THERE.
NO, I SEE HIM, TOO. IT'S ARCANE.
MOMMY, I DON'T LIKE THIS PLACE. I WANT TO GO HOME.
I KNOW, SWEETIE. ME, TOO.
I'VE SEEN THOSE THINGS, TOO. I HAVE... A CONNECTION TO IT... THE ROT, THE SAME WAY ALEC DOES TO THE GREEN AND YOUR DAUGHTER DOES TO THE RED. IT'S--IT'S IN MY BLOOD.
YOU...YOU'RE A PART OF THESE THINGS THAT HURT MY BABY!? ONE OF THEM?!
THESE THINGS HAVE BEEN TRYING TO KILL ME, TOO. SINCE I WAS A CHILD. YOU'RE NOT THE ONLY VICTIM HERE, LADY, SO BACK OFF.
PLEASE. WE MUST NOT FIGHT AMONGST OURSELVES.
THE ROT IS AS ESSENTIAL TO LIFE S THE RED AND GREEN E. BUT IT IS GROWING OUT OF CONTROL... REACHING INTO THIS WORLD WHERE IT HAS NO PLACE TO BE.
YOU'RE RIGHT, BAKER.
IT WON'T STOP COMING FOR US. WE'VE WEAKENED IT, WE'VE BEATEN IT BACK... NOW IS THE TIME TO STRIKE AT ITS HEART.

I DON'T THINK YOU SHOULD, DADDY. I THINK YOU SHOULD STAY HERE WITH US. WE SHOULD STAY *TOGETHER.*
IT'S GOING TO BE OKAY, LITTLE WING.
ME AND SWAMP THING ARE GOING TO GO DOWN THERE AND BEAT UP THE BAD GUYS, THEN EVERYTHING'S GONNA BE OKAY. I PROMISE.
NO! DON'T GO! PLEASE, DADDY! DON'T LEAVE US!
MAXINE!
LET GO, MAXINE.
YOU BETTER COME BACK TO US, BUDDY BAKER. WE NEED YOU.
I NEED YOU.
I WILL, BABY. I PROMISE.
ARE YOU SURE ABOUT THIS, ALEC? I ONLY JUST GOT YOU BACK.
YOU KNOW THIS IS WHAT I MUST DO...EVERYTHING THAT HAS HAPPENED...IT HAS ALL LED US TO THIS MOMENT.
I SHOULD COME WITH YOU. THIS WHOLE THING... I CAN'T HELP BUT FEEL IT'S MY FAULT.
NONSENSE. THIS HAS BECOME BIGGER THAN YOU OR ANY OF US, ABBY, BUT I FEAR THAT IF YOU WERE TO ENTER THE ROT, IT WOULD *NEVER LET YOU GO.* IT IS TOO DANGEROUS.
WELL, THEN, HURRY BACK. I'LL BE WAITING.
NOTHING COULD KEEP ME FROM YOU AGAIN, ABBY.

WELL, SWAMPY...YOU READY TO DO THIS?
YES...BUT I HAVE AN IDEA.
I WILL ROOT US TO THIS WORLD...KEEP US *ANCHORED.*
SO THAT WE SHOULD FIND OUR WAY BACK.
GOOD IDEA. UNFORTUNATELY, I DON'T THINK I CAN SPROUT ANY BLOOD VESSELS JUST YET.
JUST STAY CLOSE TO ME.

HERE WE GO...
SPLOOSH
THEY ARE GONE.
NOW WHAT?
NOW? NOW WE WAIT.
AND WE BE READY FOR *ANYTHING.*
CHAK

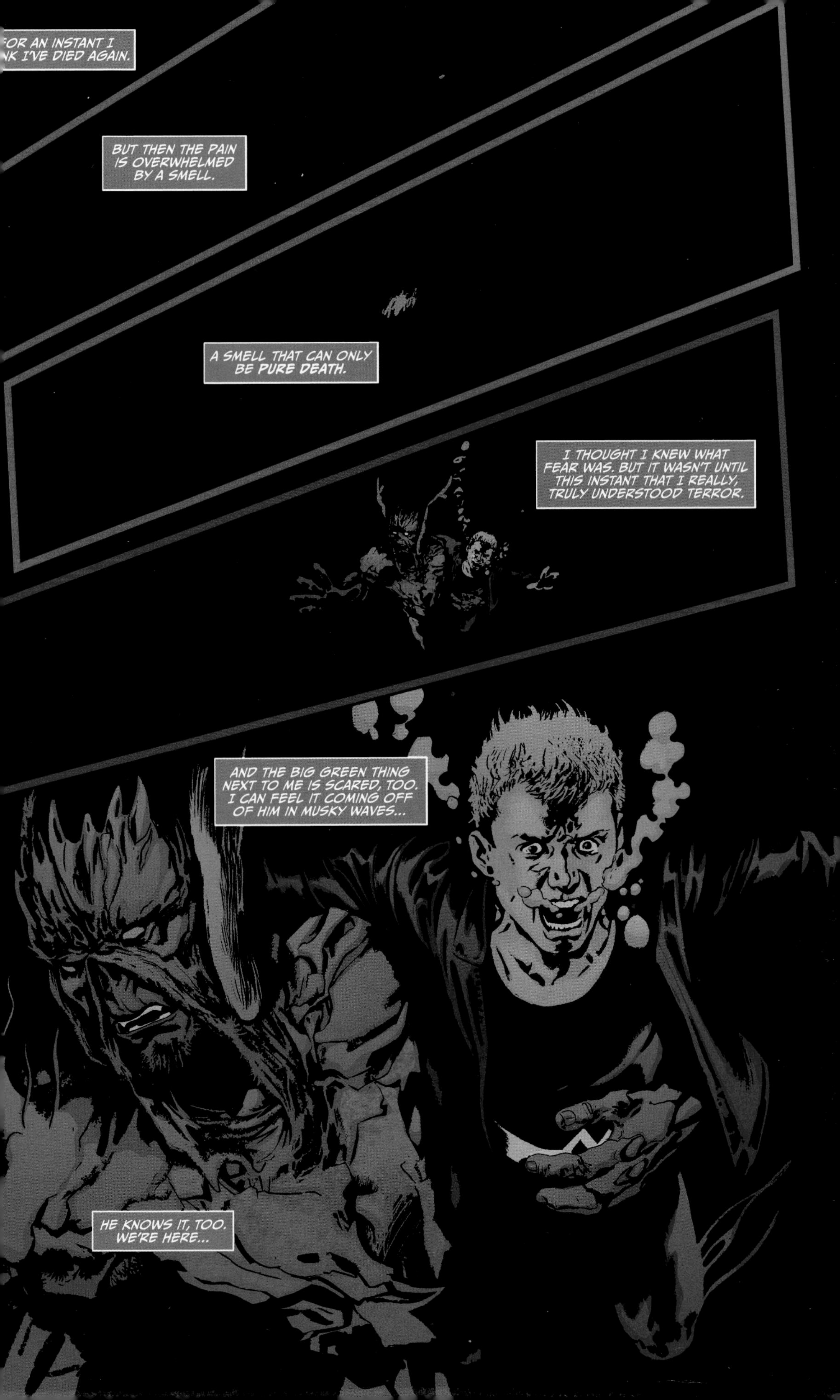
FOR AN INSTANT I NK I'VE DIED AGAIN.
BUT THEN THE PAIN IS OVERWHELMED BY A SMELL.
A SMELL THAT CAN ONLY BE PURE DEATH.
I THOUGHT I KNEW WHAT FEAR WAS. BUT IT WASN'T UNTIL THIS INSTANT THAT I REALLY, TRULY UNDERSTOOD TERROR.
AND THE BIG GREEN THING NEXT TO ME IS SCARED, TOO. I CAN FEEL IT COMING OFF OF HIM IN MUSKY WAVES...
HE KNOWS IT, TOO. WE'RE HERE...

...WE ARE IN THE ROT!

...IT'S COMING. IT'S COMING. IT'S COMING...
ROTWORLD IS COMING. ROTWORLD IS COMING. ROTWORLD IS COMING.
ROTWORLD IS COMING.
WHAT DID YOU SAY, HONEY?
SOMETHING IS WRONG.
LOOK--THE PORTAL--

--MAXINE, YOU'D BETTER GET BACK--
MOMMY!
SSSSSO IT BEGINSSSSS.

PAQUETTE
NF
2012

SCOTT SNYDER & JEFF LEMIRE
writers

MARCO RUDY
penciller

MARCO RUDY, DAN GREEN & ANDY OWENS
inkers

YANICK PAQUETTE & STEVE PUGH
cover artists

WE DID IT. WE'RE INSIDE THE ROT.
YES. BUT CAN YOU FEEL IT?
THIS WORLD OF THEIRS...IT GOES DEEPER AND DEEPER. IT'S LIKE WE'RE STANDING ON TOP OF IT, AND THIS IS JUST THE OUTER LAYER.
Not yoUr HoMe!
Go AwAy!

ROTWORLD
PROLOGUE: PART 2
GeT aWaY fROM hErE!!!
THE UN-MEN.
QUITE THE WELCOMING COMMITTEE.

MeAn
n! MEAn
--ACK!
WHAT ARE THESE THINGS? THEY'RE NOT LIKE THE HUNTERS...I CAN FEEL A TOUCH OF RED IN THESE, THEY'RE MORE--
HUMAN. THEY'RE HUMANS WHO WORSHIPPED THE ROT IN LIFE.
THIS IS HOW THEY WERE REWARDED.
SCHLUNK
LUCKY THEM.
LuCKy Un-mA--uNh!
SSLSH
BAKER. LOOK...
A TEAR IN THE ROT.
THEIR WAY UP, OUR WAY DOWN...
ALEC, ARE YOU WORRIED THIS SEEMS A LITTLE EASY?
I WORRY ABOUT ALL OF IT...
BUT THERE'S NO TURNING BACK NOW.

THE PORTAL TO THE ROT.
SSSSSO IT BEGINSSSSS.
MOMMY, CAN I USE MY POWERS NOW?
YES!!
YOU LITTLE ROTLINGS NEED A TIME-OUT!
FWOOSH
ELLEN, CATCH!
BUT ABBY, WHAT ABOUT YOU?
I CAN HANDLE MYSELF.
SSSSSSS
APPARENTLY.
BLAM

ABBY! YOU MUST USE YOUR ONNECTION TO THE ROT O SEAL THE PORTAL, OR THE ROTLINGS WILL OVERRUN US!
BUT WHAT ABOUT ALEC AND BUDDY? THEY'LL BE TRAPPED DOWN THERE!
JUST E SURE TO AL AROUND THE VINE. AS LONG THEY HAVE AMP THING'S THER, THEY HOULD BE LE TO FIND THEIR WAY BACK.
I HOPE YOU'RE RIGHT.
MAXINE, ELLEN, COVER ME.
SSSHHLLP
OKAY, ALEC.
I'M SEALING IT UP...

"...I HOPE YOU KNOW WHAT YOU'RE DOING DOWN THERE."
SEE YOU ON THE OTHER SIDE.
A LADDER OF BONE...?
GRAB HOLD!
AH!
BAKER! USE YOUR POWERS! FLY!
I...
I CAN'T!

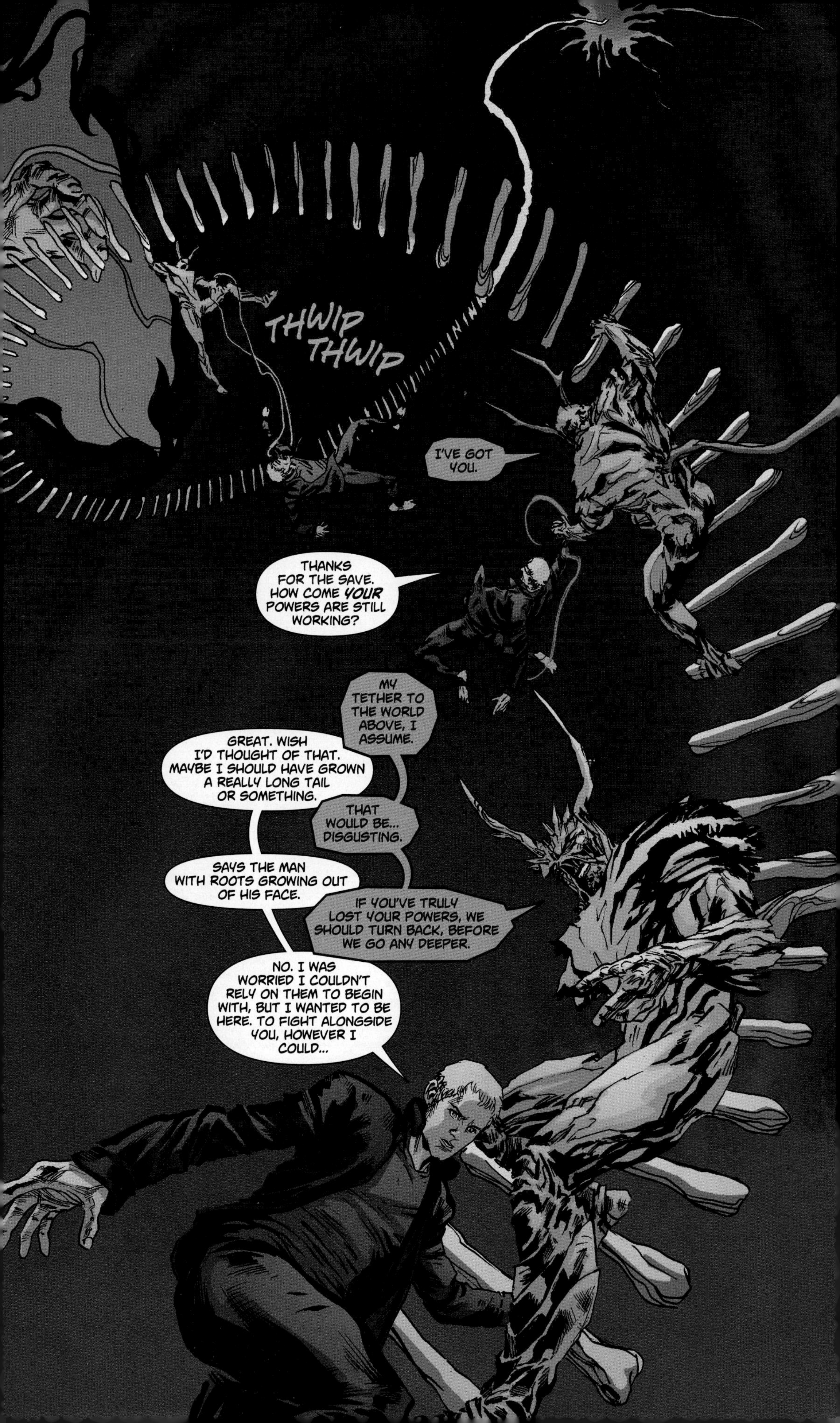
THWIP THWIP
I'VE GOT YOU.
THANKS FOR THE SAVE. HOW COME ***YOUR*** POWERS ARE STILL WORKING?
MY TETHER TO THE WORLD ABOVE, I ASSUME.
GREAT. WISH I'D THOUGHT OF THAT. MAYBE I SHOULD HAVE GROWN A REALLY LONG TAIL OR SOMETHING.
THAT WOULD BE... DISGUSTING.
SAYS THE MAN WITH ROOTS GROWING OUT OF HIS FACE.
IF YOU'VE TRULY LOST YOUR POWERS, WE SHOULD TURN BACK, BEFORE WE GO ANY DEEPER.
NO. I WAS WORRIED I COULDN'T RELY ON THEM TO BEGIN WITH, BUT I WANTED TO BE HERE. TO FIGHT ALONGSIDE YOU, HOWEVER I COULD...

"...AFTER ALL, THIS IS MY FAMILY THAT'S AT STAKE HERE."
SO... YOU'RE REALLY CONNECTED TO THE ROT?
YES. I GUESS YOU COULD SAY I WAS BORN INTO IT. THE SAME WAY I ASSUME MAXINE WAS.
SHE'S A LUCKY GIRL, THOUGH, TO HAVE FAMILY LIKE YOU AROUND.
THE BAD MAN FROM MY DREAM. HE'S YOUR FAMILY, ISN'T HE?
ANTON ARCANE, YES. THE BAD MAN. HE'S MY UNCLE.
YOUR UNCLE? BUT--
HE'S ALSO A POWERFUL SERVANT OF THE ROT. PERHAPS THE MOST POWERFUL OF ALL.
HE WAS ITS AVATAR, LIKE ALEC IS FOR THE GREEN. BUT HE DIED LONG AGO. HOW HE'S MANAGED TO COME BACK NOW AND TAKE THE MANTLE OF THE AVATAR AGAIN, I JUST DON'T KNOW...
ONCE AN AVATAR DIES, THERE SHOULD BE NO BRINGING THEM BACK.

"IT DOESN'T AKE ANY SENSE..."
KEEP GOING, BAKER. I CAN FEEL THE ROT'S FEAR.
I FEEL IT TOO, LIKE A SHIVER IN THE LADDER...
STILL, IT'S SO *QUIET*. I'M USED TO THE ROT TOSSING EVERYTHING AND THE KITCHEN SINK AT ME.
ANYWAY, YOU BEAT BACK THAT MONSTER IN THE DESERT...
SETHE, AN ANCIENT GUARDIAN OF THE ROT.
AND I TOOK DOWN THE HUNTERS THREE.
IT'S AS WE SAID IN THE SWAMP. THE ROT HAS BEEN COMING FTER US AND OUR OVED ONES FOR AS LONG AS WE CAN REMEMBER.
NOW--WHEN THE ROT IS WEAK FROM ITS BATTLES WITH US--MIGHT BE THE ONLY CHANCE WE GET TO HIT IT HARD, RIGHT WHERE IT LIVES, BEFORE IT CAN ATTACK US AGAIN.
HANG ON. DO YOU FEEL THAT?
SOMETHING'S *FOLLOWING* US DOWN THE LADDER--

ARCANE!!
HELLO, ALEC. SO NICE OF YOU TO BRING A FRIEND ALONG... I'VE BEEN LONELY DOWN HERE ALL ALONE.
I ADMIT, IT WAS EASIER THAN I THOUGHT TO GET YOU THIS DEEP INTO MY PLACE OF POWER...
WITH ONLY THIS TINY LITTLE VINE AS A LIFELINE.
ALEC, STOP HIM-- HE'S GOING TO CUT THE VINE--!
NO TIME--I'M SENDING ABBY A MESSAGE--
OH, YES... PLEASE DO WHAT YOU CAN TO WARN MY DARLING LITTLE NIECE.
BUT DON'T WORRY, HOLLAND...

"I'LL MAKE SURE SHE'S TAKEN CARE OF..."
THE VINE, IT'S--IS IT...SPELLING SOMETHING?
MOMMY, ABBY, LOOK!
OH, NO...

THE TETHER IS BROKEN! THEY ARE GONE! I CAN NO LONGER SENSE BUDDY BAKER.
IT'S OKAY, SWEETHEART. HE'LL...COME BACK. HE WILL.
LET'S JUST GET BACK TO THE HOTEL AND GET GRANDMA AND CLIFF AWAY FROM HERE, OKAY?
AND ALEC...I CAN'T FEEL HIM EITHER. ALL I FEEL IS THE ROT... ITS JOY.
IT'S GETTING STRONGER. I'M STRONGER NOW, TOO.
NO... DADDY...

THEY'RE TRAPPED DEEP, AREN'T THEY?
YES...I BELIEVE THEY ARE. TOO DEEP TO RETURN, I'M AFRAID. WITHOUT THAT TETHER, THEY WILL BE LOST IN THE ROT.
BEFORE ALEC WENT IN, I SAW SOMETHING IN THAT PORTAL. SOMETHING TERRIBLE. A VISION OF THE WORLD TRANSFORMED BY THE ROT. EVERYTHING DEAD, TWISTED.
I HAVE HAD THIS VISION, TOO.
SO THIS IS IT, THEN. THIS IS WHERE IT BEGINS.
THIS IS WHERE IT HAS ALREADY BEGUN, I'M AFRAID. NOW THE ROT'S HIVE-MIND, THE PARLIAMENT OF DECAY, WILL ALLOW THEIR FORCES INTO THIS WORLD, IN AN ATTACK THE LIKES OF WHICH HASN'T BEEN SEEN IN CENTURIES.

BUT IF WE STOP THE PARLIAMENT...
WE CANNOT, CHILD. THE PARLIAMENT OF DECAY HAS REMAINED FOREVER HIDDEN FROM THE GREEN AND THE RED. NO ONE KNOWS WHERE--
I DO.
YOU... KNOW? HOW?
I KNOW EXACTLY WHERE IT LIVES.
SOMEHOW I'VE ALWAYS KNOWN. AND I'M GOING TO STOP IT ONCE AND FOR ALL.
WHERE IS IT?
IT'S FAR AWAY FROM HERE... SOMEWHERE ONLY I CAN GO.

YOU AND YOUR FAMILY ARE WELCOME TO STAY HERE, IN THE SWAMP. MY HOUSE IS--
NO. WE'LL BE NE. THANK YOU, THOUGH.
YOU'RE GOING TO NEED A SAFE PLACE--
HA. DOES SUCH A THING EVEN EXIST ANYMORE?
WHERE ARE WE GOING TO GO, MOMMY? HOW WILL DADDY FIND US?
WE'RE GOING TO GET YOUR BROTHER, SWEETIE. DADDY WILL FIND US BECAUSE YOU AND CLIFF, YOU'RE HOME TO HIM.
AND HE ALWAYS COMES HOME. YOU KNOW THAT.
ARE YOU SURE, ELLEN?
YOU CAN SAVE THE WORLD... I JUST WANT TO SAVE MY FAMILY.
"I'M AFRAID I HAVE SOME BAD NEWS FOR YOU, MY FRIENDS..."

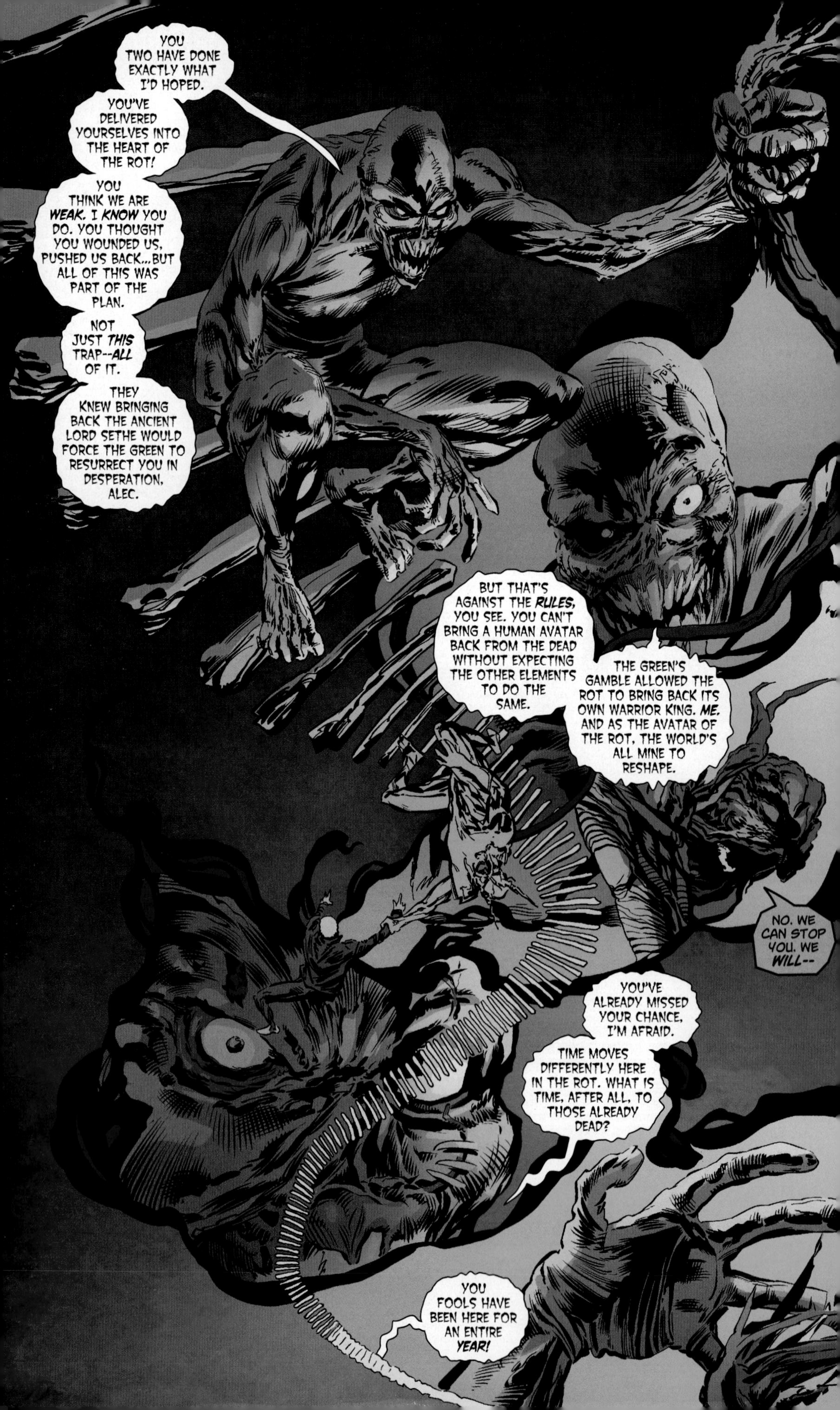
YOU TWO HAVE DONE EXACTLY WHAT I'D HOPED.
YOU'VE DELIVERED YOURSELVES INTO THE HEART OF THE ROT!
YOU THINK WE ARE *WEAK*. I *KNOW* YOU DO. YOU THOUGHT YOU WOUNDED US, PUSHED US BACK...BUT ALL OF THIS WAS PART OF THE PLAN.
NOT JUST *THIS* TRAP--*ALL* OF IT.
THEY KNEW BRINGING BACK THE ANCIENT LORD SETHE WOULD FORCE THE GREEN TO RESURRECT YOU IN DESPERATION, ALEC.
BUT THAT'S AGAINST THE *RULES*, YOU SEE. YOU CAN'T BRING A HUMAN AVATAR BACK FROM THE DEAD WITHOUT EXPECTING THE OTHER ELEMENTS TO DO THE SAME.
THE GREEN'S GAMBLE ALLOWED THE ROT TO BRING BACK ITS OWN WARRIOR KING. *ME*. AND AS THE AVATAR OF THE ROT, THE WORLD'S ALL MINE TO RESHAPE.
NO. WE CAN STOP YOU. WE *WILL*--
YOU'VE ALREADY MISSED YOUR CHANCE, I'M AFRAID.
TIME MOVES DIFFERENTLY HERE IN THE ROT. WHAT IS TIME, AFTER ALL, TO THOSE ALREADY DEAD?
YOU FOOLS HAVE BEEN HERE FOR AN ENTIRE *YEAR*!

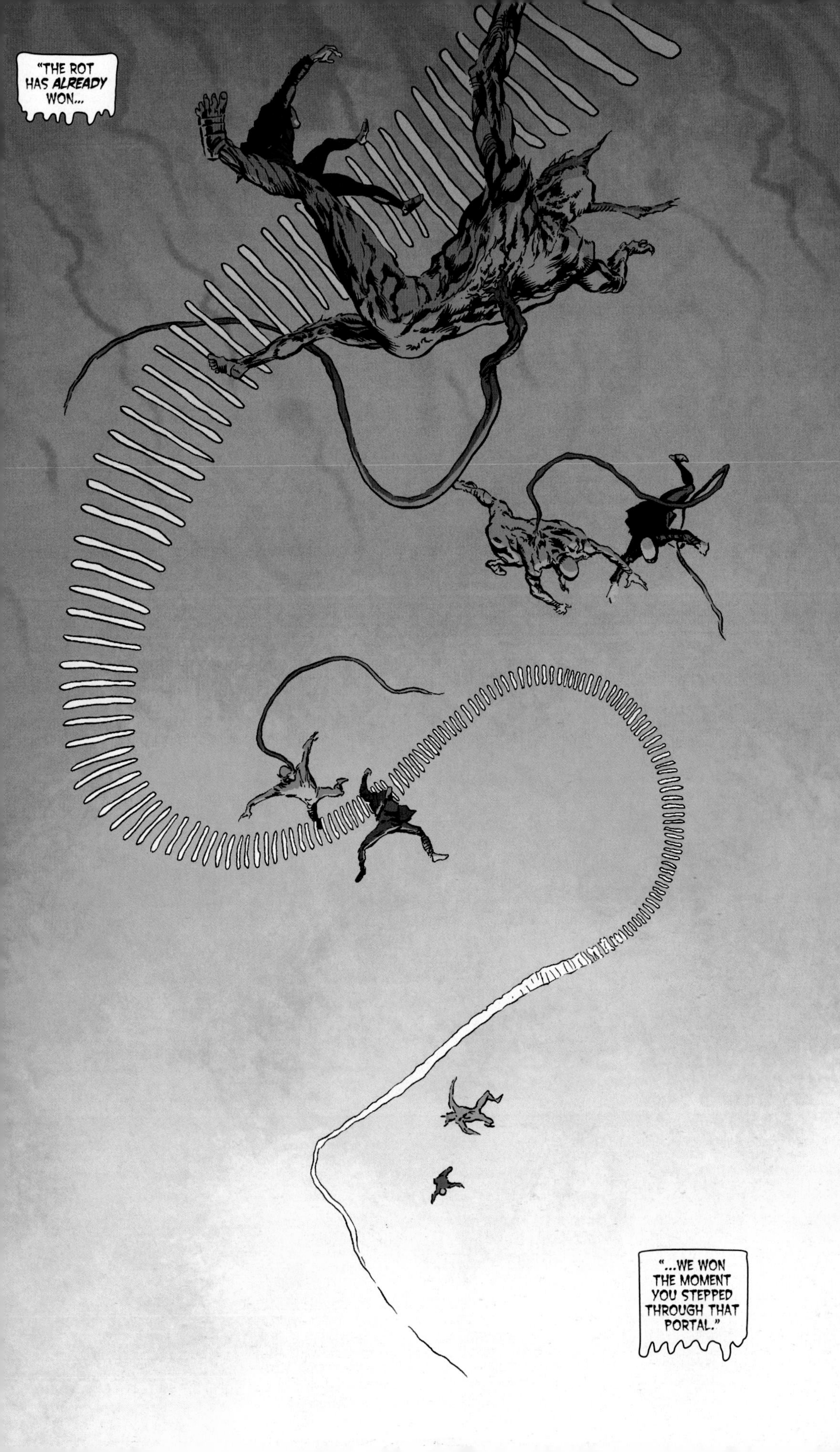
"THE ROT HAS ALREADY WON...
"...WE WON THE MOMENT YOU STEPPED THROUGH THAT PORTAL."

I FALL...
...AND FALL...
...FOR WHAT FEELS LIKE DAYS. THEN SUDDENLY IT STOPS...
...AND I'M ALONE. AT FIRST I THINK I'M IN SOME NEW, DESOLATE LAYER OF THE ROT...

...BUT I CAN FEEL THE RED AGAIN. IT'S WEAK, BUT IT'S THERE...
...BUT I CAN FEEL THE GREEN AGAIN. IT'S WEAK, BUT IT'S THERE...
AND I CAN FEEL ITS FURY. ITS BETRAYAL.
AND THAT'S WHEN I REALIZE ARCANE WAS TELLING THE TRUTH...

...THIS ISN'T THE ROT ANYMORE...
THIS IS HOME.
AND THE ROT HAS DESTROYED IT ALL.

JOSEPH SILVER additional inks STEVE PUGH cover artist

IT WAS ALL A TRAP. AND IN OUR ARROGANCE WE FELL FOR IT...
WHUMP
AND THEN KEPT ON FALLING.
AT FIRST I THINK I'VE LANDED IN SOME DEEPER LEVEL OF THE ROT...
...BUT IT'S NOT. IT'S SOMETHING FAR WORSE.

I KNOW WHERE I AM.
I'M BACK ON EARTH. THIS IS HOME.
BUT EVERYTHING'S DEAD. I REACH OUT TO TRY TO FIND AN ANIMAL TO CONNECT WITH BUT THERE IS NOTHING. I CAN FEEL THE RED, BUT IT'S WEAK.
WHAT ABOUT ELLEN AND THE KIDS? I LEFT THEM BEHIND IN LOUISIANA.
NONE OF THIS MAKES ANY SENSE AT ALL.
WAIT A MINUTE. WHAT'S THAT?
A BIRD?
NO. NOT A BIRD...
TOO BIG.

WHA
UNGH!
H-HAWKMAN!?
KRUNK
HAWKMAN, STOP! I DON'T KNOW WHAT'S HAPPENED TO YOU, BUT MAYBE I CAN HELP!?
SSSSSs...

HAVE IT YOUR WAY--!
WOARRGG...
URG!
WHA-!?
HEAD'S UP, HAWKY.

THE GOOD GUYS ARE HERE.
ROTWORLD:
THE RED KINGDOM part on

NOT SO FAST, UGLY!
UH-OH!
UH...A LITTLE HELP, GUYS!?
GWOOOOAR!
WITH PLEASURE.
SKRTCH
SPLAT
WHOA!

THAT WAS-- DISGUSTING. WHO THE HELL ARE YOU GUYS?
I AM--I WAS-- JOHN HENRY IRONS STEEL. THE FURBA IS GARFIELD LOGA BEAST BOY, AND T SHAPE-SHIFTING BEA IS BLACK ORCHI SO, WHO ARE YOU, CHIEF?
WHOEVER HE IS, THEY SENT ONE OF THE BIG GUNS AFTER HIM...NOT JUST UN-MEN AND ROTLINGS. AND THEY'LL SEND MORE SOON. WE SHOULD MOVE.
HOW'D YOU SURVIVE OUT HERE THIS LONG ON YOUR OWN, ANYWAY?
I--I JUST GOT HERE.
UH--OKAY. BUT YOU NEVER ANSWERED THE QUESTION. WHO THE HELL ARE YOU?
I'M BUDDY BAKER... ANIMAL MAN.
WHAT?
I THINK WE BETTER TAKE YOU BACK WITH US.
WHERE ARE WE GOING?
WHERE? WHERE ELSE IS THERE? WE'RE GOING BACK TO THE RED.

UISIANA. BEFORE ROTWORLD.

I CAN, MOMMY...BUT I FEEL ONE OF THE ROTTEN GUYS TOO. THEY'RE TOGETHER!
WHERE ARE YOU GOING? WE SHOULD WAIT FOR BUDDY!
I'M DONE WAITING FOR BUDDY.
I'M GOING TO GET MY SON BACK, THEN WE'RE GETTING OUT OF HERE!
LET'S GO!

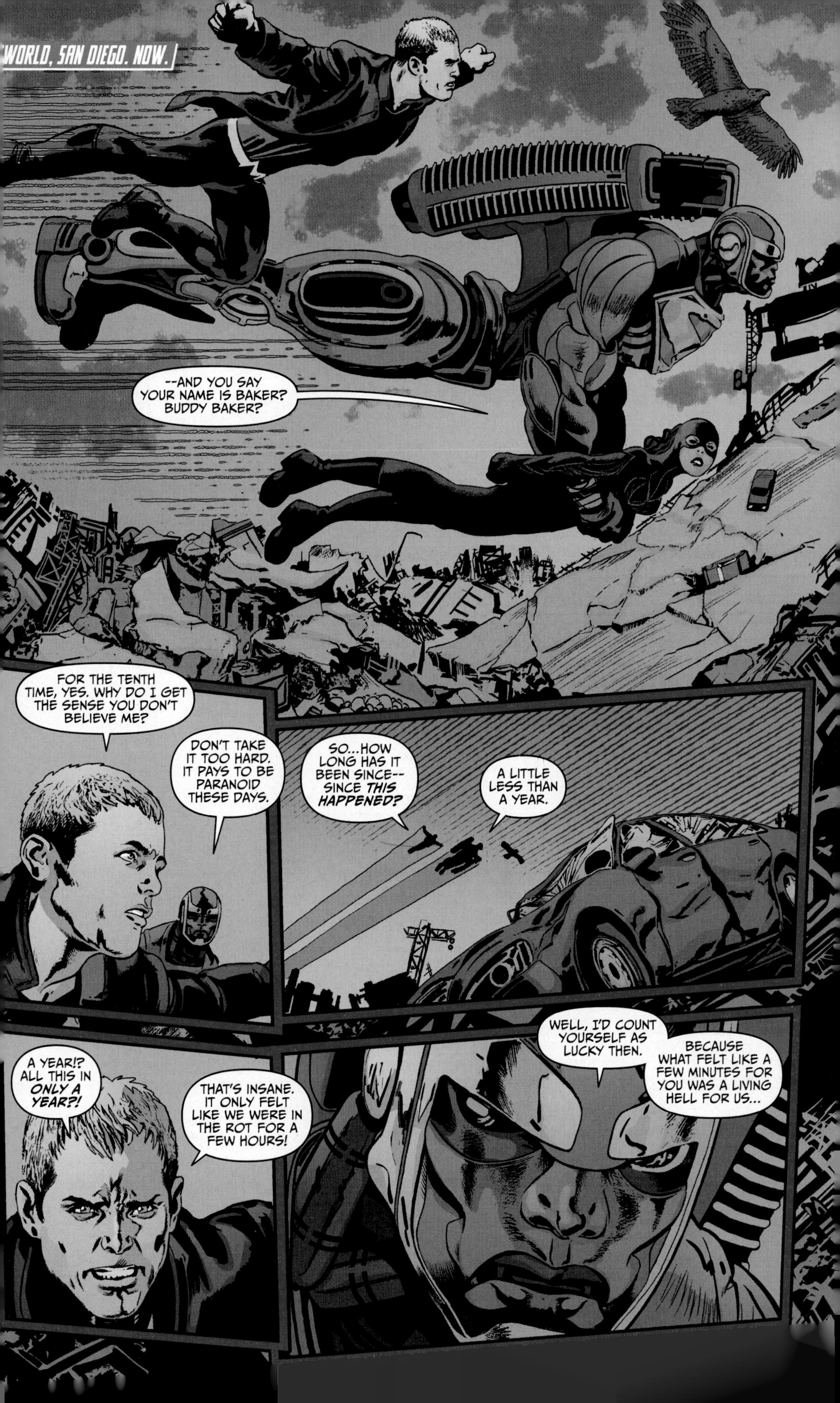
WORLD, SAN DIEGO. NOW.
--AND YOU SAY YOUR NAME IS BAKER? BUDDY BAKER?
FOR THE TENTH TIME, YES. WHY DO I GET THE SENSE YOU DON'T BELIEVE ME?
DON'T TAKE IT TOO HARD. IT PAYS TO BE PARANOID THESE DAYS.
SO...HOW LONG HAS IT BEEN SINCE--SINCE *THIS HAPPENED?*
A LITTLE LESS THAN A YEAR.
A YEAR!? ALL THIS IN *ONLY A YEAR?!*
THAT'S INSANE. IT ONLY FELT LIKE WE WERE IN THE ROT FOR A FEW HOURS!
WELL, I'D COUNT YOURSELF AS LUCKY THEN.
BECAUSE WHAT FELT LIKE A FEW MINUTES FOR YOU WAS A LIVING HELL FOR US...

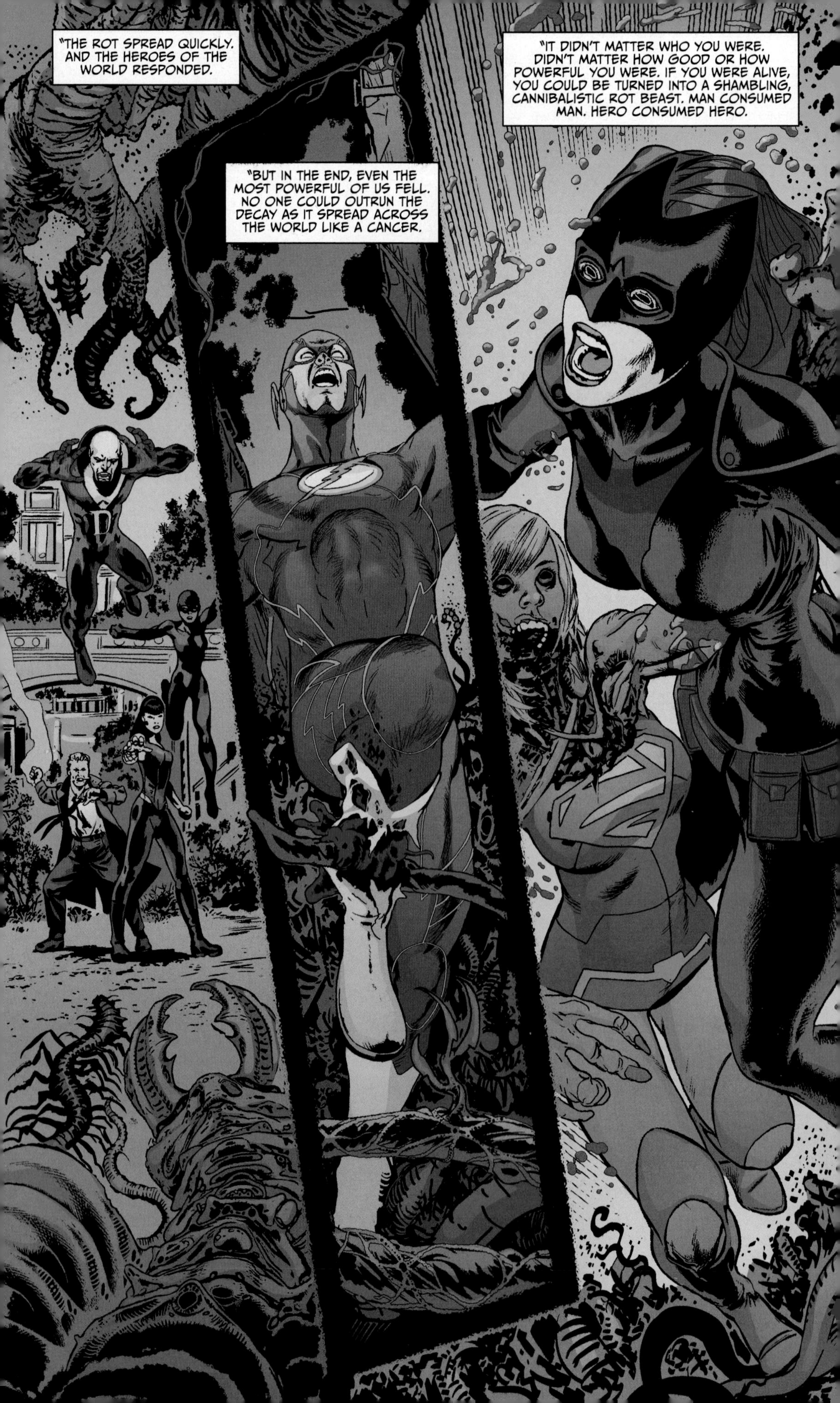
"THE ROT SPREAD QUICKLY. AND THE HEROES OF THE WORLD RESPONDED.
"BUT IN THE END, EVEN THE MOST POWERFUL OF US FELL. NO ONE COULD OUTRUN THE DECAY AS IT SPREAD ACROSS THE WORLD LIKE A CANCER.
"IT DIDN'T MATTER WHO YOU WERE. DIDN'T MATTER HOW GOOD OR HOW POWERFUL YOU WERE. IF YOU WERE ALIVE, YOU COULD BE TURNED INTO A SHAMBLING, CANNIBALISTIC ROT BEAST. MAN CONSUMED MAN. HERO CONSUMED HERO.

"I KNEW IT WAS ONLY A MATTER OF TIME UNTIL MY NUMBER WAS UP, SO I BUILT THIS WAR ARMOR AND TRANSFERRED MY CONSCIOUSNESS INTO ITS A.I.--MADE SURE THERE WAS NO FLESH LEFT FOR THE ROT TO POSSESS.
"AND OTHERS, LIKE BEAST BOY, WHO HAD SOME CONNECTION TO THE RED OR THE GREEN, AND A FEW ANOMALIES LIKE MYSELF, BECAME THE LAST HOLDOUTS AGAINST ARCANE'S GROWING ARMY.
"I MEAN, EVERYTHING WAS TURNED INSIDE OUT, MAN. EVEN SOME OF THE SCUM WHO USED TO BE VILLAINS HAD NO CHOICE BUT TO PITCH IN AND MAKE A STAND.

ALL RIGHT, ENOUGH WITH THE HISTORY LESSON, STEEL. WE'RE HERE...
WELCOME TO THE RED KINGDOM.
MY GOD!

BEFORE ROTWORLD.
IT'S GETTING DARKER. HARD TO SEE BEYOND THE TREELINE. I HOPE WE DON'T PASS BY HIM.

MOMMY!
WHA--?

OH, GOD!

CLIFF? BABY, WHAT HAPPENED? ARE YOU OKAY?
SSSSSS!
AHHH!

SSSOORRRRRR...
OH, GOD!

SSSOORRRRRR...
MAXINE, GET BACK IN THE VAN!
MOMMY!

SSSOOOOORRRYY, MOMMY.

ROTWORLD.
WHO BUILT THIS?!
THE TOTEMS... WHO DO YOU THINK?
THE TOTEMS?! WHERE ARE THEY? I NEED TO SEE THEM!
YOU ARE SEEING THEM.
WHAT? I--I DON'T UNDERSTAND.
THIS CITY... THIS ENTIRE PLACE WAS THE TOTEMS.
IN ORDER FOR THE RED TO SURVIVE, THEY TRANSFORMED THEMSELVES INTO A LIVING CITY OF FLESH AND BONE...A REFUGE FOR THE LAST SURVIVORS.
THEY'RE NOT SENTIENT ANYMORE, BUT THEIR POWER KEEPS THIS PLACE ALIVE.

BUTTER BAKER, BLONDIE MAN?!
SHEPHERD!
WELL, I WOULDN'T BE TELLIN' NO FIBBERS IF I SAID I DIDN'T THINK I'D EVER BE SEEIN' YER MUG AGAIN!
IT'S GOOD TO SEE YOU TOO, BIG GUY. I'M STILL TRYING TO FIGURE EVERYTHING OUT-- WHERE ARE MAXINE AND CLIFF AND ELLEN?!
OH, BLONDIE MAN...I'M SO SORRY...
NO...

AFRAID SO, BAKER.
NOT TO POINT ANY FINGERS, BUT AS YOU CAN SEE, THE WORLD WENT INTO THE TOILET THE MINUTE YOU AND THE BIG SALAD DISAPPEARED. I'D SAY YOU'VE GOT SOME EXPLAINING TO DO.

ONSTANTINE? TELL ME THIS IS OME TRICK-- SOME ALTERNATE IMENSION OR SOMETHING? MY AMILY...CLIFF, ELLEN, MAXINE. THEY CAN'T JUST ***BE GONE?!***

DON'T YOU GET IT, MATE?! THIS IS IT. ***THIS IS ALL THERE IS.*** THE BLOODY ROT HAS ALREADY WON!

NO! MAXINE WAS TOO POWERFUL!
SHE ***WAS*** POWERFUL... BUT SHE WAS JUST A LITTLE GIRL.

SHE WAS DOOMED THE MOMENT YOU LEFT...
SHE WASN'T READY TO DO IT ON HER OWN. AND NOW SHE'S GONE!

"YOU DIDN'T DO YOUR BLOODY JOB! YOU DIDN'T PROTECT HER!"
CLIFF, STOP!

SSSSSTOP?

I--I CAN'T STOP, MOMMY...?

M-MOM? I DON'T KNOW WHAT'S HAPPENING! I'M SCARED!
IT'S OKAY, BABY...I'VE GOT YOU. I'M GOING TO FIND A WAY TO MAKE YOU BETTER.

UNGH!
CLIFF?!

HUUURK!
OH, GOD!

HUUURK!

BLAARG!

MOMMY!

DOESSSN'T IT TASSSTE GOOD, MOMMY?

SSSSO SSSSSWEET!

JEFF LEMIRE
writer

STEVE PUGH
artist

TIMOTHY GREEN II
additional pencils

JOSEPH SILVER
additional inks

STEVE PUGH
cover artist

LOUISIANA. BEFORE ROTWORLD.
AAARRGH!
GET BACK, CHILD.
MOMMY!

E-ELLEN?
ST-STAY AWAY, MOM... SSSOMETHINGSS WRONG...

SSSSSPREADING...
ELLEN, NO!
ROTWORLD:
THE RED KINGDOM part two

MOMMY! STOP HURTING GRANDMA!
STOP IT!

MAXINE, IT IS NO LONGER SAFE HERE...WE MUST RUN!
NO! THAT'S MY MOMMY! AND I CAN'T LEAVE GRANDMA AND CLIFFY!

YOUR MOMMY ISSSS GOING AWAY, LITTLE RED THING...
AND WE'RE COMING BACK...
THE HUNTERSSSSS RETURN.

RUN, CHILD!

THE ROT HAS WON! THE FORCES OF DECAY ARE NOW FREE TO SPREAD ACROSS THE EARTH!

TWORLD. THE RED KINGDOM, SAN DIEGO. NOW.
SO JUST WHERE HAS THE LATE, GREAT "ANIMAL MAN" BEEN ALL THIS TIME, ANYWAY? CARE TO ENLIGHTEN US, BAKER?
I--WE... SWAMP THING AND I...WE WERE IN THE ROT.
BUT IT WAS SOME KIND OF TRAP. ARCANE WAS THERE...HE WAS-- HE WAS HORRIBLE, SO STRONG NOW THAT HE'S THE AVATAR OF THE ROT. AND WE FELL. I DON'T REMEMBER MUCH AFTER THAT. I WOKE UP HERE.
SO WHERE'S THE SWAMP THING NOW?
I DON'T KNOW. WE MUST HAVE BEEN SEPARATED SOMEHOW AS WE FELL.
HMMM...IF YOU RETURNED NEAR THE RED BECAUSE YOU'RE POWERED BY THE FORCE CONNECTING ALL ANIMAL LIFE, SWAMPY WAS LIKELY DRAWN CLOSER TO THE GREEN, THE CONCENTRATION OF THE ONLY REMAINING PLANT LIFE.
IF WE CAN BRING BAKER HERE AND SWAMPY TOGETHER, WE MIGHT ACTUALLY HAVE A FIGHTING CHANCE.
A FIGHTING CHANCE?! WHAT'S LEFT TO FIGHT FOR, CONSTANTINE? MY ENTIRE FAMILY IS GONE!
YEAH, WELL, WE'RE NOT! I'M REALLY SORRY ABOUT YOUR FAMILY, BUT WE ALL LOST SOMEONE.
AND THESE PEOPLE ARE STILL ALIVE, BAKER! AND IF THERE'S SOME WAY OF--
THOOM
WHAT THE HELL?
WE'RE IN ONE MESS A' TROUBLE NOW, BLONDIE MAN!
WHO THE HELL IS IT!?
WHO DO YOU BLOODY THINK?!

ARCANE'S SENT A DAMNED ARMY AFTER YOU!
HE KNOWS YOU'RE HERE NOW AND HE WON'T REST UNTIL YOU'RE DEAD.
HE HAS HORDES OF ROTLINGS AND UN-MEN AT HIS DISPOSAL, MORE THAN STEEL, BLACK ORCHID, BEAST BOY AND *WE* CAN HANDLE.
YOU'LL BE THE DEATH OF US ALL, BAKER!

TAKE THE POWER OF A PANDA OR SOMETHING AND START PUNCHING, BAKER!
THIS IS INSANE!
YEAH, WELL, YOU BETTER GET YOUR HEAD IN THE GAME, MATE, 'CAUSE WE GOT INCOMING!
WHAM
UNGH!
TOLD YOU.
SO IT'S TRUE, CONSTANTINE...YOU'VE FOUND THE LOST ANIMAL MAN.

WELL, WELL... *FELIX FAUST.* WHAT WOULD AN ASSAULT ON A MAGICAL KINGDOM BE WITHOUT AN EVIL WIZARD, EH?
I DIDN'T EXPECT MUCH. STILL, ALLYING WITH ARCANE IS LOW, EVEN FOR YOU, FAUST!

you and your merry men would be smart to join us, constantine. together we could rule the rotlands!
SOME PEOPLE WOULD DO ANYTHING TO SAVE THEMSELVES, BUDDY. TRUST ME, FAUST *ISN'T THE ONLY* TURNCOAT!
THUK
SPLIT
ARE YOU TELLING ME THAT CREEP ACTUALLY VOLUNTEERED TO JOIN ARCANE?!

YEAH, BUT MOST OF THE HEROES AND VILLAINS ARE JUST SHAMBLING MONSTERS NOW.
THEY LOST ANY SENSE OF WHO THEY WERE THE MOMENT THE ROT POSSESSED THEM.
KINDA FEEL BAD FOR THEM. THEN AGAIN, I NEVER REALLY LIKED YOU ANYWAY, GRIFTER. THIS'LL LOOK GOOD ON MY TROPHY WALL.
EH?
SSSSSSS
I'VE GOT YOU COVERED, FURBALL.
SPLAT!
DO THEY ATTACK LIKE THIS OFTEN?
NO. THEY AREN'T USUALLY THIS ORGANIZED. IT'S LIKE CONSTANTINE SAID, ARCANE MUST KNOW YOU'RE BACK!
RRROOOARGGG!

CLOSE THE GATES, CROCO-MAN! WE CAN'T BE A-LETTIN' ANY OF THEM ROTTEN BUGGERS IN!
AYE, SHEPHERD, SIR!
HEADS UP, BUTTER BAKER!
THANKS, SHEPHERD.
THOOM
HE'S A PARTICULARLY UGLY ONE, AIN'T HE? ONLY ONE WAY TO DEAL WITH THESE BEASTIES... TOUGH LOVE!
SCHLUCK
IT'S OVER, FAUST. YOU'VE LOST.
oh, but, constantine, this war was over long ago... the rot has won! the rot has won!
Besides, I did not come here to invade. I simply came to deilver a message.
a message to you, Buddy Baker. a message for the fabled Lost animal man!

OH YEAH... WELL, I'M NOT LOST ANYMORE. SO WHAT IS IT YOU HAVE TO SAY TO ME?
We have her.
WHO!? WHO DO YOU HAVE?!
Who do you think, Baker? Your precious "Little Wing"!
WHERE!? WHERE IS MAXINE!?
She's in Arcane's castle.
If you want her...come and get her, big man.
See you soon...
BASTARD!
EASY, BLONDIE MAN... EASY.

WELL, I'D SAY THAT WAS ABOUT THE MOST OBVIOUS TRAP EVER LAID.
OF COURSE IT'S A DAMN TRAP. BUT I DON'T CARE! I HAVE TO GO!
EVEN IF YOUR GIRL'S ALIVE, YOU'LL NEVER MAKE IT.
ONCE YOU GET OUT THERE IN THE ROTLANDS, YOU'LL BE EXPOSED. EVEN WITH ALL YOUR POWER, YOU'LL NEVER SURVIVE ON YOUR OWN. ARCANE WILL HAVE YOU JUST WHERE HE WANTS YOU.
JOHN, YOU SAID IT YOURSELF. IF WE CAN FIND SWAMP THING, WE MIGHT ACTUALLY HAVE A CHANCE OF TAKING ARCANE DOWN!
AND THEN WHAT? THE WORLD'S SCREWED.
THEN? I DON'T KNOW, MAYBE WE START TO REBUILD. MAYBE WE DIE TRYING. EITHER WAY, STAYING HERE AND JUST SURVIVING IS NOT ENOUGH ANYMORE!
ORCHID'S RIGHT! I MEAN, WE'RE SUPPOSED TO BE THE HEROES, RIGHT?
I'M WITH BEAST BOY. LET'S GO AFTER THEM FOR A CHANGE.

I KNOW IT'S A SUICIDE MISSION. BUT IF THERE IS EVEN A CHANCE THAT MAXINE IS ALIVE, THEN I *HAVE* TO GO.
AND WHAT ABOUT ALL OF THESE PEOPLE? ARE WE JUST SUPPOSED TO LEAVE THEM HERE UNPROTECTED?
ME AN' MY DOGGIE FRIENDS'VE KEPT THE RED SAFE FOR A LONG TIME, HELLBLAZER...WE SURE AS HECK CAN DO IT NOW.
'SIDES, IF BUTTER BAKER BLONDIE MAN STAYS HERE, HE'S JUST GONNA BRING MORE AN' MORE BEASTIES TILL THEY GET US ALL ANYHOW.
IT'S SETTLED, THEN. WE GATHER SUPPLIES AND LEAVE AT SUNSET. THE SOONER WE GET MOVING THE BETTER.
BLOODY FINE MESS THIS IS.
BET YOU WON'T ALL BE SO EAGER FIGHT WHEN YOU FI OUT *WHO'S GUARD* ARCANE'S BLOOD CASTLE.

BEFORE ROTWORLD.
MAXINE... COME OUT. WE MISSSSS YOU...
MAXINE, WE MUST GO! WE CANNOT LET THEM FIND US!
MAXINE!

I--I CAN'T.

I--I DON'T WANNA RUN ANYMORE. I HAVE TO HELP MY MOMMY AN' GRANDMA AND CLIFF.
OH, CHILD... I KNOW IT IS HARD TO UNDERSTAND WHAT IS HAPPENING, BUT YOU CANNOT HELP THEM.

THE ROT IS GROWING. EVEN NOW I CAN FEEL IT SPREADING THROUGH THIS WORLD. WITH THE SWAMP THING AND YOUR FATHER GONE, THERE IS LITTLE CHANCE OF STOPPING IT.
BUT, WHAT LITTLE HOPE IS LEFT LIES WITH YOU, MAXINE. YOU ARE THE AVATAR OF THE RED, THE HUMAN DEFENDER OF THE FORCE CONNECTING ALL ANIMAL LIFE.

BUT I'M ONLY LITTLE. I CAN'T DO ANYTHING! WHY DON'T YOU TURN INTO A GREAT BIG CAT AGAIN? THEN MAYBE YOU CAN HELP ME.
IT TAKES AN INCREDIBLE AMOUNT OF POWER TO TRANSFORM INTO MY TOTEM-SELF. I CANNOT DO THAT AGAIN FOR SOME TIME.
LISTEN TO ME, MAXINE, YOU MAY BE YOUNG, BUT THE RED HAS MADE YOU WISE **BEYOND YOUR YEARS.** YOU ARE LIKE NO FOUR-YEAR-OLD I'VE EVER KNOWN.
THEY HAVE ATTACKED YOUR FAMILY TO DRAW YOU OUT...TO MAKE YOU WEAK. YOU CANNOT GO BACK TO THEM NOW UNLESS YOU ARE WILLING TO **KILL THEM.**
KILL THEM!?
I COULD NEVER HURT MY MOMMY AND CLIFF!

WELL, THEN YOU HAVE NO CHOICE BUT TO RUN. BECAUSE IF YOU CAN'T KILL THEM, THEY WILL NEVER STOP HUNTING YOU!

MAXINE, WHERE ARE YOU?
THEY DRAW CLOSER!

COME OUT AND PLAY WITH USSSSSSS.... WE MISSSSSS YOU.
WE NEED TO MOVE! NOW!

WHAT HAPPENED HERE?
THE ROT IS SPREADING, MAXINE.

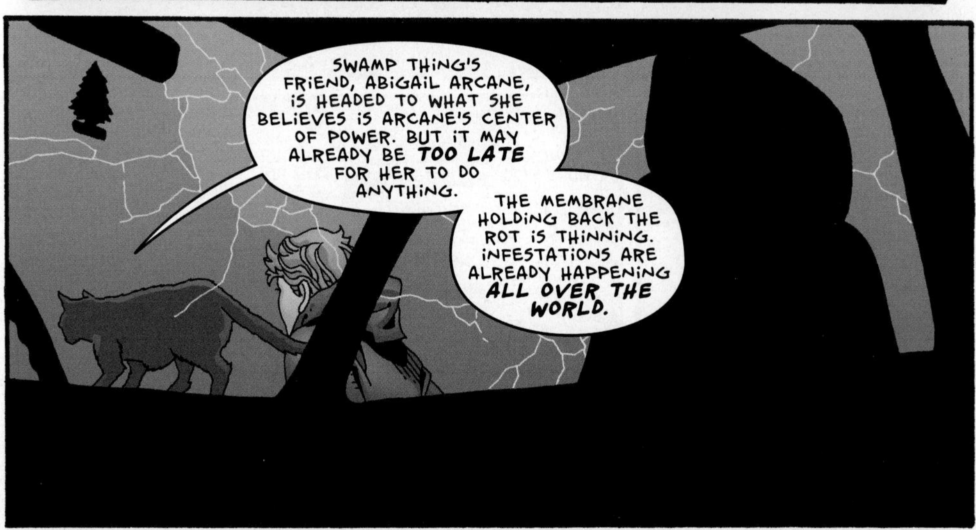
SWAMP THING'S FRIEND, ABIGAIL ARCANE, IS HEADED TO WHAT SHE BELIEVES IS ARCANE'S CENTER OF POWER. BUT IT MAY ALREADY BE TOO LATE FOR HER TO DO ANYTHING.
THE MEMBRANE HOLDING BACK THE ROT IS THINNING. INFESTATIONS ARE ALREADY HAPPENING ALL OVER THE WORLD.

THEN HOW DO WE STOP IT?
WE DON'T. NOT ON OUR OWN. WE NEED TO FIND ALLIES. CONSTANTINE, MAYBE? WOODRUE?

MAYBE THEN WE CAN BEGIN TO--

SHHH!

I HEAR SOMEONE!
MAXINE, SOMETHING IS NOT RIGHT HERE...

NO, SILLY... IT'S JUST A LITTLE BOY.
P-PLEASE DON'T HURT ME.

I WON'T HURT YOU.
YOU--YOU'RE NOT ONE OF THOSE THINGS? THOSE MONSTERS?
NO. I'M THE AVATAR OF THE RED AND MY DADDY IS A SUPER HERO. YOU DON'T NEED TO BE SCARED.

I'M MAXINE. WHAT'S YOUR NAME?
MY NAME IS WILLIAM... *WILLIAM ARCANE.*

OTWORLD. CENTRAL CITY. NOW.
--YOU GUYS SURE WE SHOULD BE STOPPING?
ME BLOODY FEET ARE KILLING ME. I CAN'T FLY LIKE YOU TOSSERS.
WHAT I WOULDN'T DO FOR A BLOODY BIT OF TOBACCO RIGHT ABOUT NOW.
IF I HAD A NICKEL FOR EVERY TIME I'VE HEARD YOU SAY THAT IN THE LAST YEAR...
WHY COULDN'T I AT LEAST HAVE HAD THE SMARTS TO END UP IN THE GREEN? AT LEAST THEN I MIGHT'VE GROWN ME A BIT, EH?

WHERE *IS* THE GREEN?
LAST WE HEARD, THERE WAS JUST A SMALL POCKET LEFT SOMEWHERE IN THE SOUTHEAST. IF YOU CAME HERE, CHANCES ARE HE'S THERE.
SO, WHAT'S YOUR STORY? ARE YOUR POWERS FROM THE RED TOO?
ACTUALLY, THEY'RE FROM THE RED *AND* THE GREEN. I GUESS I'M SORT OF A HYBRID.
HOW IS THAT POSSIBLE? IT DOESN'T SEEM... NATURAL?
IT'S NOT. NOT REALLY.
BEFORE ALL THIS...DID YOU EVER HEAR OF SOMETHING CALLED THE TAPROOT PROJECT?
NO. WHAT IS--
UH, GUYS... DO YOU SMELL THAT?

WHAT IS IT? ROTLINGS?
NO. THAT'S JUST IT. IT DOESN'T SMELL LIKE THE ROT AT ALL. IT SMELLS LIKE...
...LIKE *ANIMALS.*
BAKER, DID YOU--
IT'S NOT ME.
ARRRGH!
JESUS!
UNGH!
UH... GUYS?
UH-OH...
IT IS POINTLESS TO RESIST. YOU LOST THIS BATTLE THE MOMENT YOU ENTERED *NEW GORILLA CITY...*

NOW TAKE A KNEE, METAL MAN...AND BOW BEFORE GRODD!

JEFF LEMIRE
writer

STEVE PUGH
artist

TIMOTHY GREEN II
additional pencils

JOSEPH SILVER
additional inks

STEVE PUGH
cover artist

ROTWORLD. CENTRAL CITY.
I SAID KNEEL BEFORE GRODD, METAL MAN!
NOT A CHANCE! STOP YOUR MENTAL ATTACK ON MY FRIENDS OR I'M GOING TO BLAST YOUR ASS BACK TO--
THE ROBOT TALKS TOO MUCH!
DESTROY IT, MALLAH!
MY PLEASURE, BRAIN!
BRATATATAA
RIP HIM APART, GORILLAS!
GET OFF!

SNIFF FUNNY, THIS ONE SMELLS...WELL, HE SMELLS LIKE *ONE OF US!*
CH-CHANNELING G-GORILLA STRENGTH... THROUGH THE RED...
SPEAK UP, HUME. ARE YOU TRYING TO ADDRESS *GRODD?*
SAID-- I'M AS-- AS STRONG AS YOU NOW...
WHUMP
MORON.
THE INSURGENTS ARE FREE OF GRODD'S CONTROL...*KILL THEM, MALLAH!*
KILL THEM A--
BRAIN!

RIDE THEM DOWN, MY LEGION! FOR THIS DAY, THESE VILE TRAITOROUS APES, AND ALL AGENTS OF THE ROT, WILL KNOW THE WRATH OF FRANKENSTEIN AND HIS PATCHWORK ARMY!
FOOM!
ROTWORLD:
THE RED KINGDOM part three

FRANCIS, OLD SON. NICE OF YOU TO FINALLY SHOW UP. SEE YOUR LITTLE ARMY'S GROWN SINCE WE LAST TALKED, EH?
FRANKENSTEIN!? ARE YOU KIDDING ME? I ALWAYS THOUGHT HE WAS JUST AN URBAN LEGEND!
HRRN...CONSTANTINE. I HAVE MADE IT MY BUSINESS TO KEEP TRACK OF WHO AND WHAT MARCHES ACROSS THESE FOUL LANDS. MY ARMY AND I HAD BEEN TRACKING YOU FOR DAYS.
AND I ASSURE YOU, ANIMAL MAN, WHILE I AM A LEGEND, I AM THE VERY REAL KIND.
FOOM!
IT IS A PLEASURE TO MAKE YOUR ACQUAINTANCE. A TRUE WARRIOR OF THE RED IS A WELCOME ADDITION.
BEAST BOY... STEEL...HOW ARE YOU LADS MAKING OUT?
NOT BAD, CON MAN. THINK YOU MIGHT WANT TO LEND A HAND?
DON'T LIKE GETTING ME HANDS DIRTY, GAR. YOU KNOW THAT.
THESE GUYS AREN'T SO TOUGH WITHOUT GRODD'S MIND CONTROL TO BACK THEM UP!
I'D SAY GRODD'S ALL OUT OF POWER.
WHUMP

A SWIFT VICTORY. LEAVE A FEW ALIVE TO SEND WORD BACK TO THE ROTTEN VERMIN WHO STILL HAUNT THIS ONCE BEAUTIFUL LAND, MY SOLDIERS.
LET THEM KNOW THAT FRANKENSTEIN IS COMING FOR VENGEANCE!
IF YOU REALLY WANT VENGEANCE, THEN JOIN US, FRANKENSTEIN!
WE'RE HEADED TO ARCANE'S STRONGHOLD, TO FINISH THIS ONCE AND FOR ALL.
MY SCOUTS SAY THE KINGDOM TOO WELL GUARDED. Y RETURN TERRIFIED WITH RUMORS OF GATEKEEPERS OF INCREDIBLE POWER.
TAKING NEW GORILLA CITY IS ONE THING, BUT TO MARCH ON ARCANE HIMSELF WOULD BE SUICIDE. WE NEED TO GATHER MORE SOLDIERS... SYSTEMATICALLY WEAKEN HIS FORCES FIRST.
THERE'S NO TIME!
JUST LOOK WHAT'S HAPPENED HERE IN ONLY A YEAR. IF WE WAIT ANY LONGER THERE WILL BE NO ONE LEFT TO FIGHT.
NO. I'VE MASTERED THE FORBIDDEN SCIENCE OF MY MAKER AND NAMESAKE, VICTOR FRANKENSTEIN. I CAN MAKE MORE PATCHWORK WARRIORS WHO ARE IMMUNE TO THIS ELEMENTAL FORCE OF DECAY, THE ROT.
NO OFFENSE, FRANCIS, BUT I DON'T HINK EVERYONE WANTS O BE TURNED INTO AN UNDEAD GHOUL JUST TO SURVIVE.
BAKER'S RIGHT. THIS IS OUR ONLY CHANCE TO STRIKE, EVEN IF OUR CHANCES ARE SLIM. AND YOUR ARMY WILL CERTAINLY HELP OUR ODDS.
IT WILL STILL NOT BE ENOUGH. UNLESS--
WHAT ARE YOU THINKING, BIG MAN?

I HEAVE HEARD A RUMOR THAT THE ROT KING, ARCANE, KEEPS A PRISON DEEP BELOW METROPOLIS. A KEEP FOR A BEING **TOO POWERFUL** TO CONVERT OR DESTROY.
IF THIS WERE TRUE...IF WE WERE TO FREE THIS PRISONER OF WAR--
METROPOLIS? WHY WOULD HE KEEP THEM SO FAR FROM HIS STRONGHOLD?
IF WHAT FRANK SAYS IS TRUE, MAYBE ARCANE FEARS WHOMEVER IT IS HE HAS LOCKED DOWN THERE...WANTS TO KEEP THEM AT A DISTANCE?
THE BATTLE THERE WAS ONE OF THE FIERCEST. THE PEOPLE OF METROPOLIS WERE ONE OF THE LAST HOLDOUTS. SUPERMAN AND I MANAGED TO HOLD THE UN-MEN OFF FOR MONTHS. AND THEN...
THEN?
THEN SUPERMAN JUST--DISAPPEARED. NO ONE SAW HIM DIE. NO ONE SAW HIM CAPTURED. HE WAS *JUST GONE* ONE DAY. THE CITY FELL SOON AFTER.
WITHOUT HIM WE COULDN'T STOP THE ROT... *I* WASN'T ENOUGH TO SAVE THEM.
YOU DON'T THINK IT COULD BE ***SUPERMAN,*** DO YOU?
NO ONE KNOWS WHAT HAPPENED TO BIG BLUE. IF THERE'S EVEN A CHANCE HE'S STILL ALIVE--
WELL, SUPERMAN OR NOT, I DON'T SEE ANY OTHER OPTION. IF ARCANE'S CASTLE IS AS WELL-GUARDED AS FRANKENSTEIN SAYS, MAYBE THIS ***MYSTERY PRISONER*** IS THE KEY.
WE ***NEED*** TO GO TO METROPOLIS!

UISIANA. BEFORE ROTWORLD.
A-ARCANE? YOUR NAME IS WILLIAM ARCANE?
THIS IS A TRAP, CHILD, WE MUST GET AWAY FROM HIM!

NO! PLEASE DON'T LEAVE ME ALONE!
MY SISTER, ABBY! YOU KNOW HER, RIGHT?

YES...WE KNOW ABBY. SHE HELPED US. BUT I--

I'VE BEEN LOOKING ALL OVER FOR HER. CAN YOU HELP ME FIND HER? I-I'M LIKE HER. I'M NOT BAD LIKE THE OTHER ARCANE.
I MEAN I WAS. I DID BAD THINGS. BUT THEN ABBY AND THE SWAMP THING STOPPED ME...MADE ME REALIZE HOW WRONG I'D BEEN.
I'VE EVEN BEEN USING MY POWER TO PROTECT PEOPLE SINCE THIS STARTED. PLEASE, YOU HAVE TO BELIEVE ME!

DO NOT LISTEN TO HIM, MAXINE. WE HAVE TO RUN NOW! YOUR MOTHER...CLIFF... THEY WILL BE HERE SOON!

YOUR MOM?
THE ROTTEN STUFF HAS THEM... I *NEED HELP.*

DOES YOUR MOM HAVE RED HAIR?! YOUR BROTHER HAS A FUNNY HAIRCUT?
YES! DID YOU SEE THEM?! DID THEY TRY TO HURT YOU?

NO, YOU DON'T UNDERSTAND! MY POWER, IT LETS ME PULL THE ROT *OUT* OF THINGS.
I *ALREADY* HELPED THEM! THE AND A FEW OTHER PEOPLE. THEY'RE BA AT AN OLD FARM JU THROUGH THE WOO RESTING WHERE IT WAS SAFE.

REALLY!? TAKE ME THERE! PLEASE?!
MAXINE!
YOU BE QUIET!

THAT'S MY MOMMY AND MY BROTHER AND MY GRANDMA! YOU CAN'T TELL ME WHAT TO DO! YOU'RE JUST SUPPOSED TO HELP ME, BUT YOU AIN'T EVEN TRIED!
MAXINE, PLEASE--

NO! I *BELIEVE* WILLIAM. LET'S GO!

IT'S JUST UP AHEAD. I'M SO GLAD I FOUND YOU, MAXINE. YOUR MOM IS GOING TO BE SO HAPPY TO SEE YOU.
ME TOO. YOU SURE THEY'RE OKAY NOW?

I PROMISE.

THIS WAY! IN THERE!

MOMMY?!

NO!
SORRY... GUESS I KINDA LIED.

YESSSS, LITTLE RED THING. IT IS USSSSSSS... THE HUNTERSSSS TWO.
YOUR FATHER KILLED OUR BROTHER HUNTER. NOW WE SSSSEEK A THIRD...
...AND THAT THIRD ISSSS YOU, MAXINE BAKER...

WORLD.
PROACHING METROPOLIS.
IT'S ALMOST SUNDOWN. WE SHOULD STOP FOR THE NIGHT. WE NEED TO TRY AND GET SOME REST. WE'LL REACH METROPOLIS SOON ENOUGH AND WE'LL NEED TO BE READY.
NEITHER MY ARMY NOR I REQUIRE SLEEP. I SUGGEST YOU RETIRE TO ONE OF OUR SUPPLY WAGONS FOR THE NIGHT. THAT WAY WE CAN KEEP MOVING.
WELL, YOU MAY NOT BE TIRED, FRANK, BUT MY HOOVES ARE KILLING ME.
YEAH, I'M EXHAUSTED. BARELY RESTED SINCE I GOT HERE.
VERY WELL, REST IN PEACE, MY FRIENDS-- I SHALL AWAKEN YOU WHEN METROPOLIS IS IN SIGHT.
YAWN "REST IN PEACE"... I THINK YOU NEED TO RETHINK YOUR PHRASING THERE, BIG BOY.
HRNN...

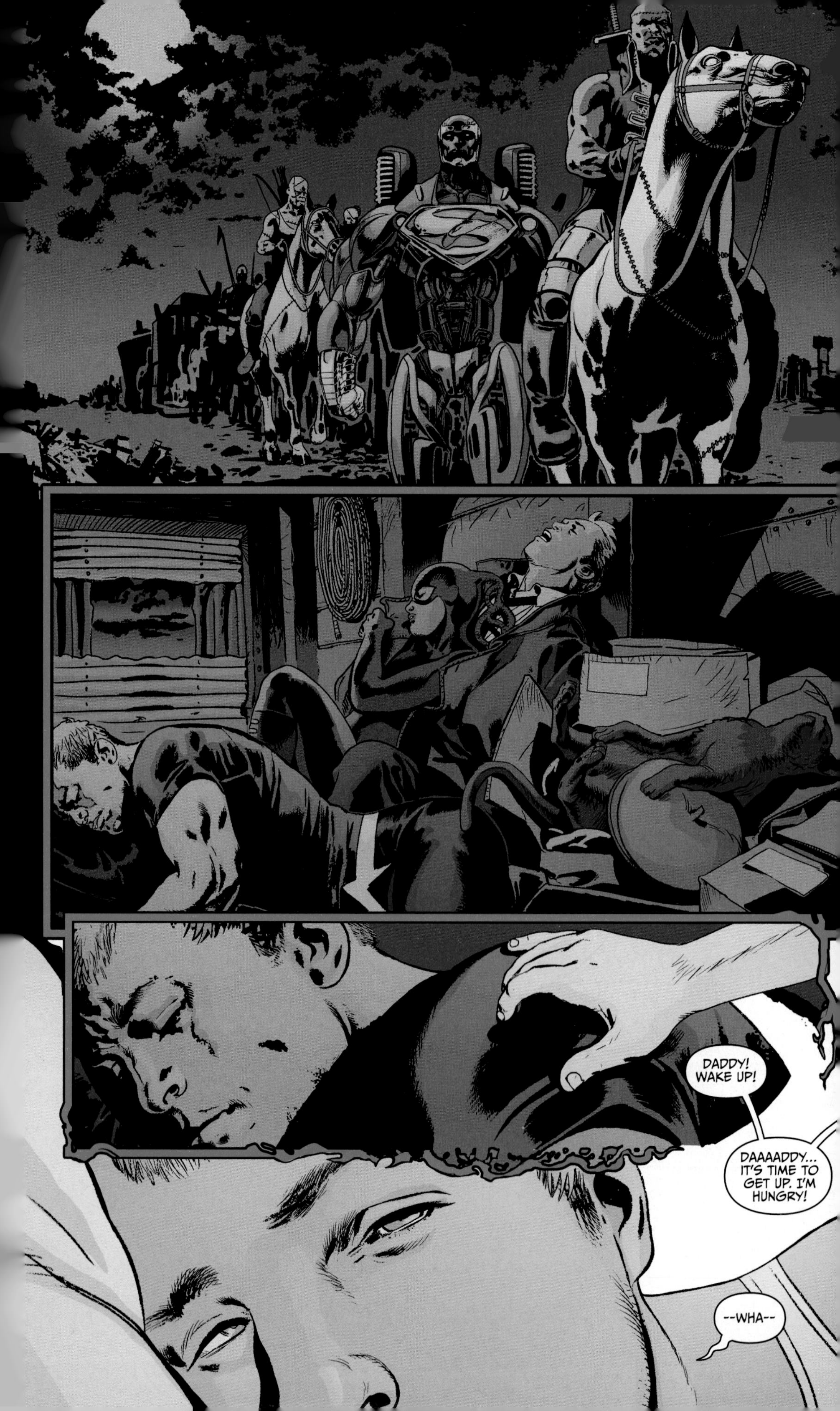
DADDY! WAKE UP!
DAAAADDY... IT'S TIME TO GET UP. I'M HUNGRY!
--WHA--

COME ON, DAD! YOU PROMISED YOU'D MAKE US VEGAN PANCAKES THIS MORNING!
S-SORRY, LITTLE WING. HAD A LATE NIGHT. CRAZY QUILT ATTACKED THE SAN DIEGO PORT AGAIN...
WHERE'S MOM?
IN THE KITCHEN MAKING YOU COFFEE, SILLY.
UMMM... COFFEE.
MORNING, HON.
EVOLVE OR DIE
HEY, SWEETIE. HOW WAS WORK LAST NIGHT?
MEH...NOT BAD. STOPPED A ROBBERY DOWNTOWN, THEN HAD TO DEAL WITH SOME RIDICULOUS GUY CALLED CRAZY QUILT. SAME OLD...
WHERE'S CLIFFY?

ELLEN? WHAT IS IT?

MAXINE? WHERE'S YOUR BROTHER? DID--DID SOMETHING HAPPEN?
HE'S IN THE BACKYARD. WHERE ELSE DO YOU THINK HE'D BE?

THE BACKYARD? WHAT'S HE DOING IN THE BACKYARD? I-I DON'T UNDERSTAND...WHAT'S GOING ON HERE?
CLIFF?
YOU BACK HERE, PAL? WHAT'RE YOU DOING OUTSIDE SO EARLY IN THE--
UNGH JESUS--
HEY, DAD!
OH, GOD!

DAD...I'M SORRY, BUT I THINK I RUINED MY COSTUME. I'LL HAVE TO GET ANOTHER ONE BEFORE OUR NEXT ADVENTURE.
C-CLIFF--? WHAT HAPPENED, SON? OH, GOD...WHAT'S GOING ON?
IT'S OKAY, DAD. I GET TO BE A HERO LIKE YOU NOW. IT'S WHAT I ALWAYS WANTED!
I JUST NEED YOU TO REMEMBER ONE THING...DON'T TURN YOUR BACK ON THE BOY. HE WON'T BE DEAD YET.
I DON'T UNDERSTAND! CLIFF, PLEASE!

JESUS...
MORNING, SLEEPYHEAD. I THINK IT'S TIME YOU WOKE UP.
WE'RE HERE IN METROPOLIS. AND I REALLY THINK YOU'LL WANT TO SEE THIS, MATE.
WHOA.
WHA-WHAT HAPPENED HERE?
DAILY PLANET

I DON'T UNDERSTAND! IF THIS REALLY IS ARCANE'S PRISON, THEN WHY THE HELL IS THE GREEN SO PRESENT?
NOT ALL GREEN IS GOOD, BAKER. GREEN AND RED ISN'T BLACK AND WHITE, MATE.
SNIFF SNIFF YEAH, STILL, THIS SEEMS STRANGE, NO?
YEAH. IT'S BLOODY WELL CREEPY, IT IS.
WELL, THERE'S ONLY ONE WAY TO FIND OUT IF SUPERMAN IS HERE SOMEWHERE. WE NEED TO FIND THE UNDERGROUND PRISON.
I SUGGEST WE FIND AN OPENING TO THE OLD SUBWAY SYSTEM... START THERE. AND QUICKLY. THIS PLACE IS GIVING ME THE CREEPS.
DAILY PLANET
BAKER IS RIGHT. THERE IS A STRANGE DARKNESS HERE...ONE THAT EXTENDS BEYOND JUST THE ROT. WE NEED TO SEE TO OUR WORK AND MOVE ON.
MY PATCHWORK LEGION AND I SHALL STAY ABOVE AND STAND SENTRY.

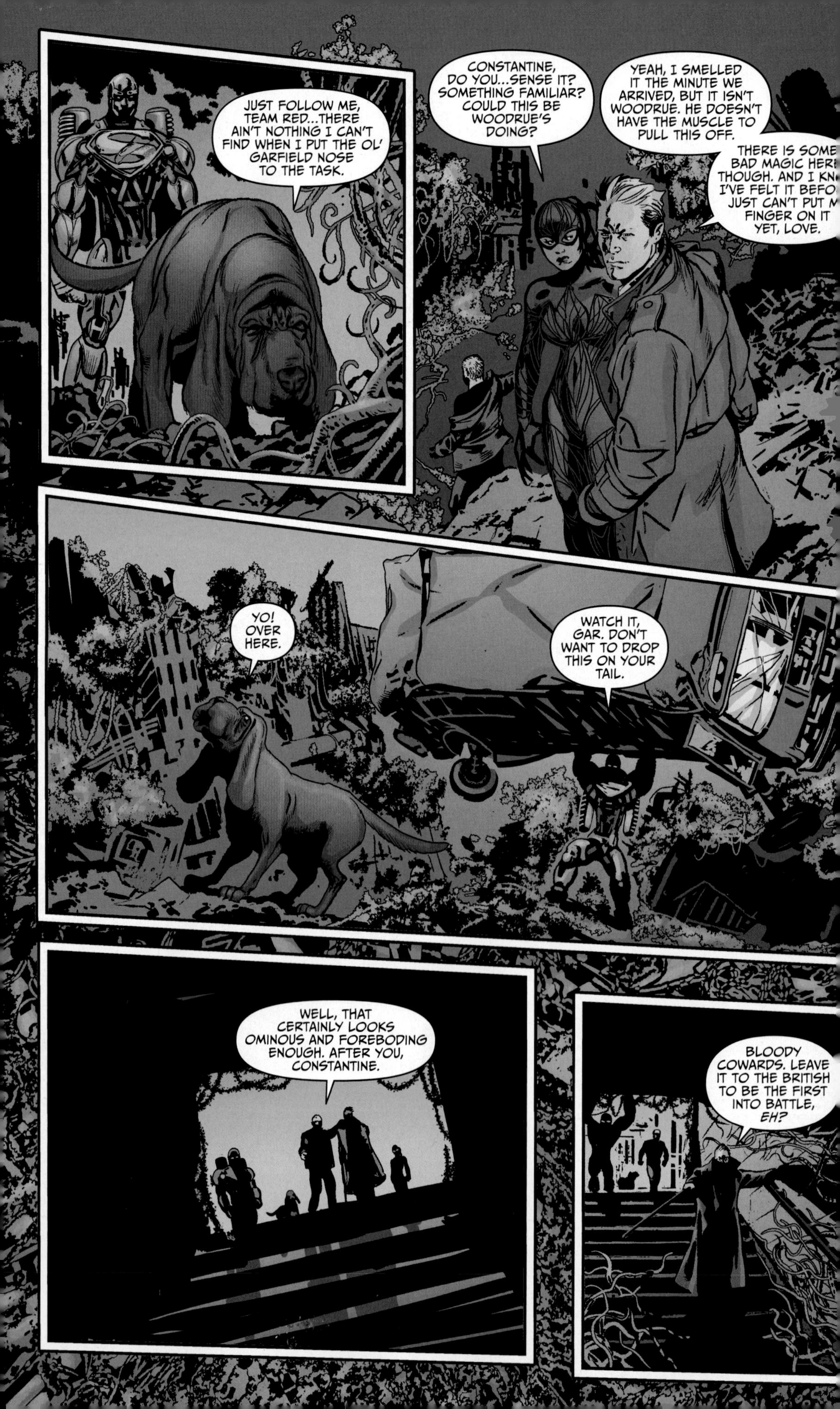
JUST FOLLOW ME, TEAM RED...THERE AIN'T NOTHING I CAN'T FIND WHEN I PUT THE OL' GARFIELD NOSE TO THE TASK.
CONSTANTINE, DO YOU...SENSE IT? SOMETHING FAMILIAR? COULD THIS BE WOODRUE'S DOING?
YEAH, I SMELLED IT THE MINUTE WE ARRIVED, BUT IT ISN'T WOODRUE. HE DOESN'T HAVE THE MUSCLE TO PULL THIS OFF.
YO! OVER HERE.
WATCH IT, GAR. DON'T WANT TO DROP THIS ON YOUR TAIL.
WELL, THAT CERTAINLY LOOKS OMINOUS AND FOREBODING ENOUGH. AFTER YOU, CONSTANTINE.
BLOODY COWARDS. LEAVE IT TO THE BRITISH TO BE THE FIRST INTO BATTLE, *EH?*

I'M PICKING UP A FAINT ENERGY SIGNATURE JUST AHEAD. I'M CROSS-REFERENCING IT WITH ANY KNOWN SUPERHUMAN SIGNATURES IN MY DATABASE...
DON'T NEED YOUR STINKING COMPUTER, STEELY. I CAN SMELL SOMEONE UP AHEAD... STRANGE MUSKY SCENT, THOUGH.
YEAH, I SMELL IT TOO.
WHOA. WELL, I GUESS WE FOUND THE PRISON.
YEAH, A BIT TOO EASILY THOUGH. STEEL, YOU PICKING UP ANY OTHER LIFE FORMS?
NO. NO ROTLINGS OR UN-MEN WITHIN FIVE HUNDRED MILES OF THE CITY. JUST THE ONE SIGNATURE. AND LIKE I SAID, IT'S FAINT. JUST BEYOND THESE "BARS." STILL HAVEN'T FOUND A MATCH, EITHER.
WELL, I'M NOT WAITING AROUND UNTIL YOU DO. LET'S JUST DO THIS AND GET THE HELL OUT OF HERE.
SLASH
IS--IS SOMEONE BACK THERE? I HEAR BREATHING, BUT IT'S WEIRD...WET AND HOLLOW.
UH, GUYS... I JUST GOT A MATCH! OH, MAN--
IS THAT--?
IT CAN'T BE!

GREEN LANTERN!?

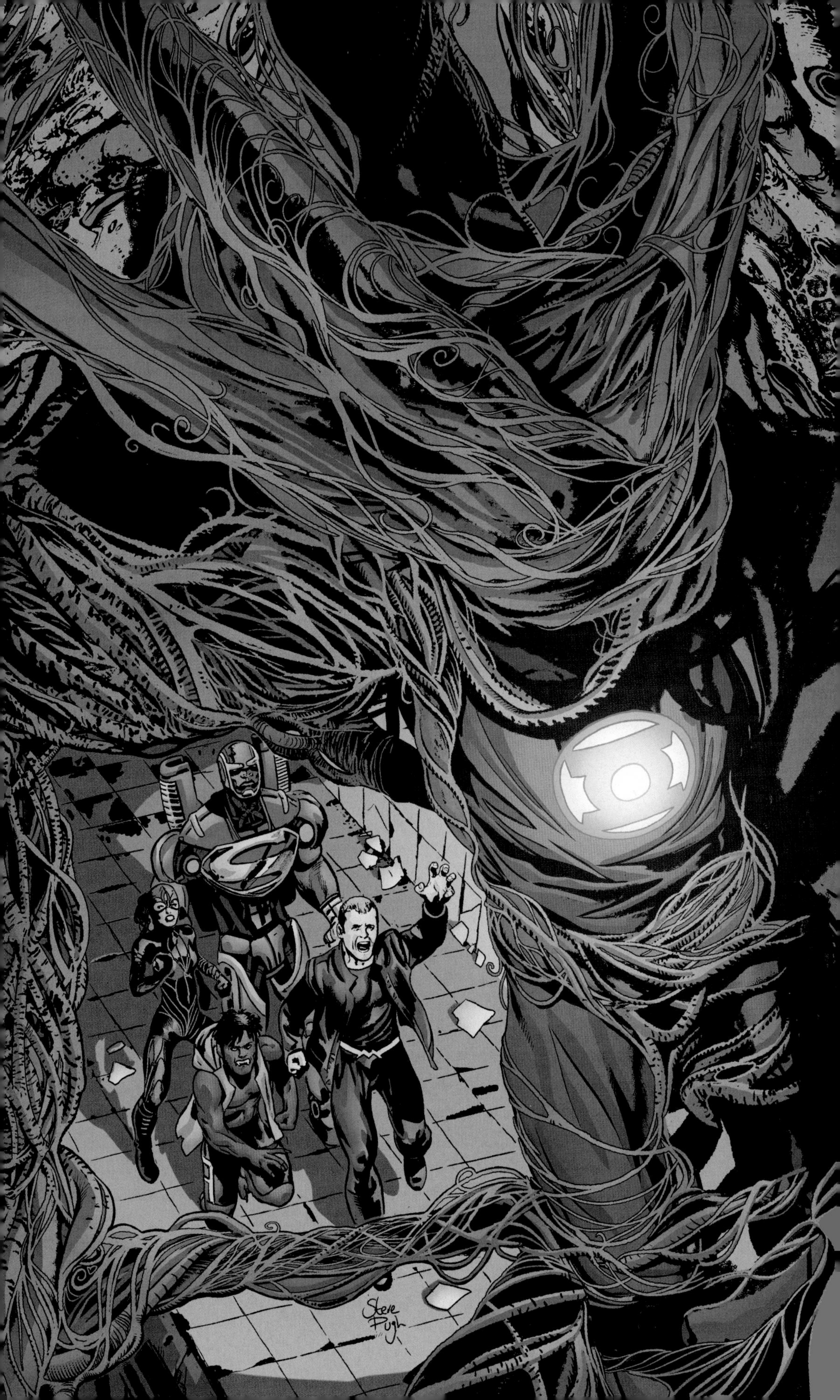
Steve Pugh

JEFF LEMIRE
writer

STEVE PUGH
artist

TIMOTHY GREEN II
additional pencils

JOSEPH SILVER
additional inks

STEVE PUGH
cover artist

I AM MEDPHYLL. GREEN LANTERN OF SECTOR 2814... PLEASE HELP ME.
ROTWORLD:
THE RED KINGDOM part four
KRRITCH
GOT HIM, BUDDY?
HOW LONG HAVE YOU BEEN DOWN HERE?
QUESTIONS LATER, STEEL, JUST HELP ME GET HIM DOWN!
BLACK ORCHID, GIVE ME A HAND!
I--I LOST TRACK OF THE DAYS MONTHS AGO...IS IT OVER? HAS THE ROT FALLEN?
I WISH IT WAS OVER. THE WORLD HAS FALLEN TO ARCANE. WE CAME HERE TO FIND YOU...WE THOUGHT YOU MIGHT BE ABLE TO HELP US STORM HIS STRONGHOLD. BUT--

YOU PLAN TO ATTACK? GOOD. I WILL BE THERE TO FIGHT WITH YOU, COMRADES. I CAN SENSE YOUR CONNECTION TO THE RED AND GREEN, BUT FIRST I NEED TO GET TO MY POWER BATTERY.
MY RING HAS BEEN LONG DEAD, BUT IF I CAN JUST RECHARGE IT--
WHOA. EASY, PAL. EASY. WHY DON'T YOU TAKE IT SLOW? HOW DID THIS HAPPEN TO YOU? AND WHERE ARE THE OTHER GREEN LANTERNS? EARTH'S GREEN LANTERNS?
YOU DON'T UNDERSTAND. I AM EARTH'S GREEN LANTERN...
S I'M SURE YOU KNOW FAR TOO WELL, WHEN THE ROT SPREAD, YOUR PLANET'S HEROES UNITED TO STAND IN ITS PATH.
"BUT, AS EVEN YOUR GREATEST CHAMPIONS FELL, THE GUARDIANS OF THE UNIVERSE KNEW THE INFESTATION COULD NOT BE STOPPED.
"THE FALL OF EARTH WAS INEVITABLE.
"BUT THE GUARDIANS, IN THEIR WISDOM, KNEW THAT THOSE BEINGS WITH A STRONGER CONNECTION TO EARTH'S ELEMENTAL FORCES-- THE RED AND THE GREEN-- MAY STAND A CHANCE.
"MY SPECIES COMES FROM A PLANET SEVEN MILLION LIGHT-YEARS FROM EARTH. WE ARE A PLANT-BASED SPECIES. AS SUCH, THEY SAW ME AS THE GREEN LANTERN WITH THE GREATEST CHANCE OF SURVIVING AND HELPING EARTH.

"SO I CAME HERE TO FIGHT. AND THEN THE GUARDIANS SEALED OFF THE PLANET.
"NOT EVEN THEIR FORMIDABLE POWER COULD PUSH BACK THE ELEMENTAL FORCES AT WORK HERE. THEIR BEST HOPE WAS TO *QUARANTINE* EARTH SO THAT THE ROT COULD NOT LEAVE THIS PLANET AND ***SPREAD OUT ACROSS THE UNIVERSE.***
"AND FIGHT I DID. AT LEAST UNTIL I WAS *IMPRISONED* DOWN HERE."
AT IS IT? T DID THIS D YOU?
NOT WHAT... ***WHOM!***
UH...GUYS. I THINK SOMETHING'S COMING!
BEAST BOY'S RIGHT. I HAVE MOVEMENT. SOMETHING BIG IS HEADED RIGHT TOWARDS US!
UH-OH. STEEL, I THINK I JUST FIGURED OUT WHAT SEEMED SO FAMILIAR...
WHO DARES!?
WHO DARES TRESPASS IN MY SACRED VEINS AND WALK MY UNHOLY ARTERIES?!
OH CRAP!

WHO DARES ENTE BLACKBRIAR THORN THE LIVING CITY!

LOUISIANA. BEFORE ROTWORLD.
MOMMY?! CLIFF? WAKE UP!
THEY ARE OURSSSS, LITTLE RED QUEEN! JOIN USSSS...

I--I CAN KILL YOU! I CAN SEND YOU AWAY! LET THEM GO!
HSSSSS!

YOU KILL USSSS HUNTERSSS, FLESHTHING, AND YOUR PRECIOUSSSS FAMILY IS LOST TO THE ROT FOREVER.
WE ARE NOT FOOLISSSH ENOUGH TO THINK WE CAN BESSST YOU IN COMBAT. YOU ARE AN AVATAR, AND EVEN A YOUNG ONE IS MUCH GREATER IN STRENGTH THAN USSSSS...
THISSSS ISSS WHY WILLIAM ARCANE LURED YOU HERE, MAXINE...WE WISSSH TO MAKE A DEAL...
YOUR LIFE FOR THE LIVESSSS OF YOUR FAMILY. A SSSSSIMPLE TRA
YOU BECOME THE TH
HUNTER. BALANCE O
RANKSSSS AND W
LET THEM GO.
DO NOT LISTEN TO THEM, MAXINE. YOU MUST RUN, NOW. AWAY FROM THESE ABHORRENT THINGS!
YOUR SAFETY IS ALL THAT MATTERS NOW! I SHOULD NEVER HAVE LET YOU COME HERE. THIS IS MY FAULT, AND MY BATTLE!
I HATE CATS. FILTHY, TRICKY. FULL OF DISEASE...
SOCKS!
HAK HAK

NO! STOP IT!
HAAOOORRK!

HA HA! OU LITTLE IDIOT!
THERE'S NOTHING YOU CAN DO TO ME! I AM AN ARCANE!
SOON MY UNCLE WILL BE LORD OF EVERYTHING! AND WHEN HE IS, HE'S GOING TO GIVE ME THE SEA!
YOU ARE A BAD, BAD LITTLE BOY! STOP HURTING MY CAT!

SSSSSTOP IT! THISSSS ISSSS YOUR LASSSST WARNING.
COME TO USSS NOW, MAXINE BAKER...OR YOUR MOTHER FALLSSSSS INTO THE DARKNESSSS FOREVER!

ROTWORLD.
THORN, YOU MAD OLD WOODEN BASTARD! YOU THINK ARCANE WILL LET YOU LIVE DOWN HERE AFTER HE'S DONE AWAY WITH THE LAST OF US?
YOU'RE DELUSIONAL, MATE. HE'LL WIPE YOU OUT THE MOMENT HE DOESN'T NEED YOU ANYMORE!
SILENCE, LITTLE MAGE! WHEN I DELIVER THE RED KING TO ARCANE, HE'LL GIVE ME WHATEVER I WANT!
SORRY, BIG BOY...BUT YOU'RE NOT THE ONLY ONE HERE CONNECTED TO THE GREEN
SKRRTT
I FEEL LIKE I'M MISSING A REAL OPPORTUNITY FOR A GOOD ONE-LINER ABOUT LOSING YOUR HAND OR SOMETHING...
I GOT YOU!
LEAVE THE WITTY RETORTS TO ME, ORCHID. JUST KEEP DOING WHATEVER THE HELL YOU'RE DOING. IT'S WORKING.
TH-THAT'S IT. THAT'S ALL I GOT. HE'S TOO STRONG. TOO BIG.

HE MAY BE HUGE, BUT IT'S ALL JUST A GIANT MANIFESTATION. INSIDE ALL THAT WOOD HE'S JUST ANOTHER MAN. A SCARED LITTLE WIZARD. WE NEED TO GET AT 'IM!
BAH! YOUR TIME HAS COME, CONSTANTINE. THAT POISON TONGUE OF YOURS HAS SPREAD ENOUGH LIES!
IF THERE IS A MAN IN THERE, I'LL FIND HIM. THE REST OF YOU NEED TO KEEP HIM BUSY.
WHAT ARE YOU THINKING, BAKER?
I'M THINKING TERMITE. A BIG ONE.
CRACK
ALL RIGHT! YOU HEARD HIM. KEEP THE BEARDED BASTARD BUSY!

WITH PLEASURE!
GUESS NO ONE BOTHERED TO TELL YOU, MR. THORN--
CHOOM! CHOOM! CHOOM!
--BUT METROPOLIS IS *MY CITY!*
ALTHOUGH THERE ARE FEW ANIMALS LEFT, I USE THE CLAWS OF A BADGER, BACKED WITH STAMINA OF AN OX AND THE RAW STRENGTH OF AN ELEPHANT, TO BURROW.
AND THE DEEPER I GET INTO HIM, THE MORE I THINK CONSTANTINE MUST BE RIGHT...
...THERE REALLY IS A MAN SOMEWHERE IN THIS MESS OF VINES AND ROOTS.
IT'S THE ***NOSE OF A LION*** *TIPS ME OFF. THERE ISN'T WOOD IN HERE...SOMEWHE CLOSE* ***THERE'S MEAT.***
WHA--!?
SORRY, LITTLE MAN...

YOU CAN'T HIDE FROM A HUNTER LIKE ME!
ROOOAARR!
WHATEVER BAKER DID, IT'S WORKING! THE OLD MAN IS WILTING!
KA-CHOOM
GOT HIM.
WELL PLAYED, BAKER.
PTOO
YEAH, AND NONE TOO SOON. I THINK I JUST SWALLOWED MY WEIGHT IN WOOD CHIPS.
YOU HANGING IN THERE, MEDPHYLL?
I-I WILL LIVE. LET US HURRY. I HID MY POWER BATTERY ABOVE BEFORE THORN CAPTURED ME...

WHOA, FRANKENSTEIN! LOOKS LIKE WE MADE IT JUST IN TIME TO JOIN THE PARTY!
HRNN...PERHAPS YOU COULD REFRAIN FROM YOUR QUIPS FOR A MOMENT AND LEND A HAND, BEAST BOY?
DAILY P
IT APPEARS AS THOUGH YOUR ACTIONS BELOW HAVE ALERTED ARCANE'S FORCES TO OUR WHEREABOUTS. WE'VE A FULL-SCALE INVASION ON OUR HANDS!
SHCLUNK
MEDPHYLL, WE COULD USE YOUR POWER, MATE. WHERE THE HELL DID YOU STASH THE BATTERY?!

LIKE YOUR FRIEND DR. IRONS, I FOUND THE ROTLINGS HAD SOME DIFFICULTY WITH METAL...I HID IT THERE... INSIDE THE GLOBE!
MOVE!
DAILY PLANET
YOU'RE UP, BAKER.
--ON IT!
THOOM
THANK YOU, FRIENDS. I WAS BEGINNING TO THINK I WOULD DIE ALONE IN THAT SUBWAY.
IN BRIGHTEST DAY, IN BLACKEST NIGHT, NO EVIL SHALL ESCAPE MY SIGHT...
LET THOSE WHO WORSHIP EVIL'S MIGHT, BEWARE MY POWER...

--GREEN LANTERN'S LIGHT!
NOW, LET ME TEACH ARCANE THAT HE WAS RIGHT TO BEWARE THE POWER OF THE GREEN LIGHT!
FWOOOOSH
DAMN! THAT IS WHAT I CALL POWER.
INDEED...BUT WHILE MY RING IS RECHARGED, I FEAR MY VEGETABLE-ANATOMY IS STILL VERY FRAIL AND WEAK. I--I MUST REST.
EASY, MEDPHYLL... YOU'VE DONE ENOUGH FOR TODAY.
WE HAVE A LONG RIDE TO ARCANE'S STRONGHOLD. SO REST UP. BECAUSE WHEN WE GET THERE IT WILL TAKE EVERYTHING WE'VE GOT TO BRING THAT BASTARD DOWN.

I--I'M SORRY, SOCKS. I CAN'T RUN AWAY. THAT'S MY FAMILY.
I'LL DO IT...AND THEN YOU CAN TAKE MY MOMMY AND CLIFF AND GRANDMA AWAY FROM HERE. BUT DON'T WORRY. MY DADDY WILL BE BACK. HE'LL SAVE ME.
NO, CHILD!

YES. MY DADDY WILL COME BACK AND MAKE EVERYTHING OKAY. I KNOW IT.

YESSSS... COME TO USSSS, CHILD...COME TO THE ROT.
DON'T BE SSSSCARED, LITTLE ONE...PURIFICATION IS SSSSO BEAUTIFUL.
UNGH...
M-MOM?

OH, CLIFF! THANK GOD YOU'RE ALL RIGHT!
MAXINE, NO!
MAXINE! WHAT ARE YOU DOING!?
IT'S THE ONLY WAY, MOMMY...
NO!
IT ISSSS ALREADY DONE...

HE ROT HASSSS WON! HE ROT HASSSS WON!
SSSSSSS!
NO! NO, THIS CAN'T BE HAPPENING!
DON'T YOU SSSSEEEEE...?
THISSSS IS HOW THE WORLD DIESSSS!

ROTWORLD. IN THE HEART OF THE DEADLANDS.
FASTER, MY FRIENDS! DAWN APPROACHES AND SO DOES THE STRONGHOLD OF ARCANE.
WE'VE NO TIME FOR REST. NO TIME FOR MERCY! THIS IS IT! THIS IS HOW THE ROT DIES!
WOW, FRANK WAS RIGHT. HIS ARMY REALLY DOESN'T GET TIRED. THEY'VE BEEN RIDING LIKE THAT FOR HOURS!
THAT'S NOT THE ONLY THING HE'S RIGHT ABOUT. THE ROT IS GETTING STRONGER. HE'S CLOSE...
I SENT THREE SCOUTS AHEAD LAST NIGHT, BUT THEY HAVE NOT RETURNED. YET I STILL SEE NO SIGN OF THESE SO-CALLED "GATEKEEPERS." ALL IS QUIET.
ARCANE!
WHAT IN NAME MELMOT
URK!
WOOOSH

WE ARE UNDER ATTACK!
BY WHAT!?
TRYING TO GET A BEAD ON IT, SEE IF I CAN GET A SHOT OF WHATEVER THE HELL IT IS. SO FAST--CHK-- OH GOD! I THINK I KNOW WHAT THAT IS!
WELL, THEN, ENLIGHTEN US, IRONS, WE'RE GETTING SLAUGHTERED HERE!
URK!
JOHN!
YOU MONSTER!
WOOOSH
THAT WAS ONLY A FIRST STRIKE TO WEAKEN OUR FORCES! THE GATES ARE OPENING!
WOOOSH
MY GOD, LOOK AT THEM ALL! STEEL, CAN YOU SEE THEM? WHAT ELSE ARE WE DEALING WITH HERE!?
OH, NO. I--I KNOW WHO THEY ARE-- THE GATEKEEPERS. I CAN SEE THEM...

MAG: x300
...IT'S THE JUSTICE LEAGUE!

Steve Pugh
NF.

JEFF LEMIRE & SCOTT SNYDER
writers

STEVE PUGH
artist

TIMOTHY GREEN II
additional pencils

JOSEPH SILVER
additional inks

STEVE PUGH & YANICK PAQUETTE
cover artists

TWORLD. THE CASTLE OF ANTON ARCANE.
THIS IS IT. IS IS THE END.
VERY CELL IN MY BODY SCREAMS. E RED, THE FORCE OF ALL ANIMAL LIFE, BUZZES THROUGH MY VEINS. THIS IS WHAT EVERYTHING HAS BEEN ABOUT. THIS MOMENT. WAR.
AND MAXINE IS IN THERE SOMEWHERE. MY BABY... MY LITTLE WING. I CAN SENSE HER POWER. IT'S LIKE A BRIGHT RED LIGHT BEHIND MY EYES.
THESE MONSTERS ARE BETWEEN ME AND HER. ARCANE'S GATEKEEPERS. ONCE THEY WERE SOME OF THE GREATEST HEROES THIS WORLD HAD EVER SEEN. NOW THEY'RE MINDLESS ABOMINATIONS.
AND I WON'T STOP FIGHTING UNTIL EVERY LAST ONE OF THEM IS DEAD!
ROTWORLD:
WAR OF THE ROT part one

UNGH!
THUMP
SSSSSS!
I ONCE ADMIRED THE WARRIOR YOU WERE, AMAZON. BUT FRANKENSTEIN HOLDS NO REVERENCE FOR THE SHAMBLING BEAST YOU'VE BECOME!
ARRGH!
SCHLUNK
RRROOORAGG...
THERE'S TOO MANY OF THEM!
DAMN IT, BAKER! THIS IS BAD!
WE HAVE TO STOP THE FLASH! HE'S MOWING US DOWN!

I KNOW, BLACK ORCHID! BUT HE'S STILL PRETTY DAMN FAST!
WELL, THEN BE FASTER, DAMMIT!
I THINK OF MAXINE. IF SHE IS SOMEHOW STILL ALIVE IN THAT CASTLE, IF ARCANE DOES HAVE HER, THEN I CAN'T GIVE UP.
I REACH OUT INTO WHAT'S LEFT OF THE RED. THE USUAL ANIMALS I'D USE FOR SPEED-- CHEETAHS, GAZELLES, SPRINGBOKS-- ARE SCARCE NOW, SO I HAVE TO DIG DEEPER.
COCKROACHES, ANTS... THE LIVING THINGS THAT THRIVE ON DEATH... THE CREATURES "BORN WITH ONE FOOT IN THE ROT," AS SOCKS WOULD SAY... I MIX THEM INTO A COCKTAIL THAT STARTS AT THE TOP OF MY SPINE AND STARTS TO MOVE DOWN...
...INTO MY LEGS!
I GOT THIS.
I'M FAST...BUT NOT FAST ENOUGH. THE ROT SEEMS TO HAVE SLOWED THE FLASH DOWN A LOT. HE'S NOT EVEN HALF AS FAST AS HE WAS REPUTED TO BE...BUT EVEN SO, HE'S STILL WAY OUT OF MY LEAGUE.
THERE! I CAN SEE HIM FOR THE FIRST TIME--I'M GAINING--HEART BEATING SO FAST--GOING TO PUNCH THROUGH MY CHEST.

AARRGGH!
--ALMOST... THERE...
GOTCHA!
THOOM
BUDDY BAKER... SOMETHING IS HAPPENING.
PANT PANT YOU THINK?!
NO. NOT JUST HERE. ON THE OTHER SIDE OF THE CASTLE. THE GREEN, BAKER... THE GREEN IS HERE!

THIS IS IT.
THE END OF THE WORLD, OR A NEW BEGINNING. ALL OF IT DEPENDS ON THIS.
I CAN FEEL THE GREEN, THE ANIMATING FORCE OF ALL PLANT LIFE, SCREAMING TO BE SAVED. THE LAST DYING SEEDS, DEEP IN THE EARTH.
BUT WHAT I HEAR ABOVE IT ALL IS HER--ABBY. I CAN FEEL HER HERE, IN THIS HORRIBLE PLACE, HER LIFE FORCE SO CLOSE. I'VE TRAVELED ACROSS THIS WASTELAND FOR HER.
NOTHING CAN STOP ME. NOT EVEN HIM.

BARBARA, NOW!
GO GREEN.
ONE OF THE ONLY PIECES OF KRYPTONITE ON THE PLANET. BATMAN STOLE IT FROM LUTHOR IN THE DYING DAYS OF METROPOLIS.
IT WAS SUPPOSED TO BE A FAIL-SAFE AGAINST A KRYPTONIAN DOOMSDAY SCENARIO...
BUT THIS WORLD, TODAY, IS FAR PAST DOOMSDAY.

WHAM
SPANNNG

RRRRRRR
SSSSSS!
SWAMPY!
SCRUNCH!

WHAT NOW? SUPERMAN'S BODY ISN'T VULNERABLE TO KRYPTONITE ANYMORE. AND EVEN DEPOWERED, HE'S TOO STRONG!
I'M THINKING.
THINK FASTER! WE ONLY HAVE SO MANY BIO-RESTORATIVE COATED BULLETS LEFT!

IF HIS BODY IS IN FULL NECROSIS, IT MEANS THAT MAYBE THE SUN...
BARBARA, SUPERMAN'S CELLS ARE ALMOST PLANT-LIKE IN THEIR NEED FOR SUN, BUT IF THAT NEED IS REVERSED BY THE ROT, IF HE'S THRIVING OFF THE REMNANTS OF HIS OWN CELLULAR STRENGTH, THEN THE SUNLIGHT MIGHT ACTUALLY BE THE THING TO TAKE HIM DOWN.
FREEZE! I NEED YOU TO FIRE AT THE CLOUDS DIRECTLY ABOVE ME ON MY SIGNAL! DIRECTLY ABOVE ME, FREEZE!
I AM BUSY.
JUST DO IT, DAMMIT!
ALEC...
PROTECT THE BOT! IT'S THE KEY!
ALL RIGHT, BIG GUY, ROUND TWO.
SSSSSS!
NOW!
NORA?

RRRRRRR
NORA!

BATGIRL! I CAN'T HOLD HIM!

FREEZE'S GUN!

PAF

WOOOSH

BOOOM
ALEC HOLLAND IT MUST BE. THE MUST HAVE COM HERE, TOO!
BAKER, CONSTANTINE SAID THAT YOU AND HOLLAND, THE SWAMP THING, WOULD NEED TO **BE TOGETHER** IF WE WERE TO HAVE A CHANCE OF BRINGING ARCANE DOWN. YOU NEED TO GET OVER THERE!
BUT I CAN'T JUST LEAVE YOU, STEEL, AND BEAST BOY... THEY'RE CUTTING US DOWN HERE!
WELL, WELL, WELL...DON'T LOOK NOW, ANIMAL MAN... BUT I'D SAY OUR ODDS JUST GOT A BIT BETTER!

SHEPHERD!
AYE, IT'S US, ALL RIGHT, BLONDIE MAN. LOOKS LIKE YA WENT AN' GOT YERSELVES IN A REAL DILLY OF A PICKLE HERE.
SEEMS LIKE YA COULD USE A HELPIN' HAND! FOR THE RED, BOYS! FOR THE RED!
THANKS, SHEP. BUT WHAT ABOUT THE RED? WHO'S GUARDING IT?
CAREFUL, BUTTER BAKER... THIS HEADLESS ONE IS A-STIRRIN'!
THLK
IF WE DON'T WIN THIS BATTLE, BLONDIE MAN...IT WON'T MUCH MATTER NO MORE ANYHOW.
I GUESS YOU'RE RIGHT.
COURSE I'M RIGHT, BLONDIE MAN...USUALLY AM. AIN'T YOU LEARNED NOTHIN' YET?
SQUITT

ALEC, ARE YOU--
COME ON, WE NEED TO GET THE BAT-BOT INTO THE SKY ABOVE THE CASTLE.
THE VERSION OF THE BIO-RESTORATIVE FORMULA *BATMAN* WAS WORKING ON, IT'S A CLOUD-SEEDER.
YOU'RE SAYING THE BOT IS--
IT'S A BOMB. WE GET IT INTO THE CLOUDS, WE BLOW IT UP, THE RAIN IT CREATES WILL BURN THIS PLACE TO THE GROUND WITH THE FORCES OF LIFE.
CAN YOU LIFT IT?
I THINK SO, THE FORMULA IN THE BANE DEVICE IS--
YAAAA!
SWISSSH

DIE!

CAN YOU STILL LIFT IT?

NO, WITHOUT THE FORMULA, MY BODY IS WEAKENING BY THE SECOND. I CAN'T DO IT ALONE, NOT WITHOUT SOMEONE AT LEAST AS STRONG AS ME.
UNNNNH!!
THEN WE CAN KISS OUR ASSES GOODBYE.

MAXINE'S CLOSE, SHEPHERD. I CAN SENSE HER!
AYE...THERE SURE AS HECK IS SOMETHIN' FAMILIAR, BLONDIE MAN... BUT UNLESS WE SQUISH OUT ALL A' THESE LITTLE ROTTEN BUGGERS, WE AIN'T GONNA GET A CHANCE TO FIND THE LITTLE WING!
"AND IT LOOKS AS THOUGH YER COMRADES AIN'T FARIN' NONE TOO WELL NEITHER!"
HOLD ON, FRANK, I'VE GOT THE WITCH!
WHAP
ROOOORGGG!
IT APPEARS NOT, BLACK ORCHID.
THANKS FOR THE ASSIST, GUYS...
LOOKS LIKE IT'S TIME FOR ROUND TWO, BIG MAN...
CHAK!
KA-CHAK!
I'M DONE PLAYING AROUND WITH YOU, CYBORG.
ROOOAARG!

SAY GOOD NIGHT.
ROARG-- *ZZTT*
NOW, BEFORE YOU DECIDE TO GROW A NEW HEAD...
chh WRRR
chh BLEEP!
SEE, WAY I FIGURE IT, I CAN SPLIT MY A.I. ACROSS MY ARMOR AND YOUR MECHANICAL HALF...
THERE! I'M IN CHARGE NOW. IN CHARGE OF YOU AND ALL THOSE WONDERFUL WEAPONS THAT HAVE BEEN GOING TO WASTE!

ROBOTS VERSUS ROTLINGS. GOTTA LOVE IT!
THOOM! THOOM! THOOM!
FWASH
FWASH

MEDPHYLL, WONDER WOMAN IS TAKING FRANKENSTEIN AND ORCHID APART! YOU NEED TO GET OVER THERE!
FEAR NOT, ANIMAL MAN. I'LL HANDLE WONDER--
--ACK!
MEDPHYLL!
RING STATUS REPORT. GREEN LANTERN 2814 DECEASED.
SNEAKY LITTLE BUGGER!
CRACK!
SPACE SECTOR 2814 SCAN FOR REPLACEMENT SENTIENT INITIATED.
REPLACEMEN SENTIENT LOCATED.
FRANKENSTEIN OF EARTH. YOU HAVE DISPLAYED GREAT COURAGE. WILL YOU ACCEPT THIS RING?
HRRN...

I ACCEPT. AND WHILE THESE HORDES OF ARCANE MAY BE MINDLESS BEASTS...
TODAY THEY SHALL KNOW FEAR!
SCHLINK
RANKENSTEIN KNOWS NO BOUNDS!
BAKER...WE HAVE THIS UNDER CONTROL. YOU NEED TO GET OVER THERE TO SWAMP THING, IF WE'RE TO HAVE ANY HOPE OF TAKING THE CASTLE!
MAY THE BLOOD OF THE DEAD GUIDE YA, BLONDIE MAN! GO GET HER... GO GET OUR LITTLE WING!

BAKER! YOU MADE IT!
YEAH, AND NONE TOO SOON BY THE LOO OF IT, BIG GUY. PLEAS TELL ME YOU HAVE A PL BECAUSE MY FORCES A BARELY STANDING O THE OTHER SIDE.
THE BATMAN PREPARED A MASSIVE WEAPON TO USE AGAINST THE ROT, BUT IT NEEDS TO BE SEEDED INTO THE ATMOSPHERE ABOVE THE CASTLE TO HAVE ANY LASTING EFFECT!
NEVER UNDERESTIMATE BATMAN, *HUH?*
WELL, I GUESS THIS IS IT, SWAMPY. LET'S GET THAT THING IN THE AIR!
BAKER. HOLLAND. THIS IS WHAT YOU BRING TO ME?
?
DAMN.

THIS PATHETIC COLLECTION OF RATS AND COCKROACHES THAT SOMEHOW SURVIVED MY WRATH?
YOU REALLY THINK THIS WILL BE ENOUGH TO FACE ME IN MY PLACE OF POWER?
ARCANE!
WELL, I HAVE WARRIORS, TOO.
NOT JUST THESE SHAMBLING FOOT SOLDIERS...REAL WARRIORS. THE ONES YOU LOVE MOST, THOSE YOU CAME TO SAVE! UNLEASHED NOW TO KILL YOU!
NO...
I-I...FROM THE MOMENT I ARRIVED IN THIS TERRIBLE PLACE, I DIDN'T WANT TO BELIEVE IT...

ABBY! WHAT HAVE YOU DONE TO HER?
SSSSS! HELLO, DADDY!
M-MAXINE!

PAQUETTE
NF

SCOTT SNYDER & JEFF LEMIRE
writers

ANDREW BELANGER
artist

YANICK PAQUETTE & STEVE PUGH
cover artists

VORLD. THE CASTLE OF ANTON ARCANE.
ROTWORLD: war of the rot part two
JOHN CONSTANTINE ONCE TOLD ME OF A CURSE CALLED "THE ETERNAL WAKING."
THE CURSED WOULD WAKE FROM A NIGHTMARE, ONLY TO FIND HE WAS IN ANOTHER NIGHTMARE, STILL DREAMING. OVER AND OVER. ENDLESS HORROR.
FOR WEEKS, BUDDY BAKER AND I HAVE TRAVELED THIS WASTELAND OF THE ROT, AN UNDEAD WORLD RULED BY MY OLDEST ENEMY, ANTON ARCANE...
...A WORLD WHERE EARTH'S GREATEST HEROES AND VILLAINS HAVE BEEN TRANSFORMED INTO MONSTERS.
WE'VE WALKED ACROSS A COUNTRY OF DARKNESS, ALL IN HOPES OF FINDING OUR LOVED ONES ALIVE, HERE AT THE END OF OUR JOURNEY.
INSTEAD, THIS IS WHAT WE FOUND.
NOW, MY FRIENDS, 'LL WATCH YOU E AT THE HANDS OF THE ONES YOU LOVE...
THE PEOPLE YOU CAME ALL THIS TO SAVE WILL TEAR YOU APART!

M-MAXINE? OH GOD. WHAT HAS HE *DONE* TO YOU?!
UNCLE ANTON HAS *SET* ME FREE, DADDY!
DON'T YOU SSSEEE? IT'S SSSSO MUCH BETTER THISSS WAY.
THE RED IS AN ABOMINATION. *LIFE* IS A *LIE*. THERE IS ONLY TRUTH IN THE ETERNITY OF DECAY.
THIS--THIS *HAS* TO BE ANOTHER OF ARCANE'S TRICKS. IT HAS TO BE. THIS IS NOT MAXINE. THIS IS *NOT* MY LITTLE GIRL!
ARCANE! WHERE IS THE *REAL* ABBY?!
THESE *ARE* THE REAL ABBY, DR. HOLLAND! THEY'RE *MADE* FROM HER...

HEH HEH HI HEH HI
TAK TAK TAK TAK
"...NURTURED THIS TIME BY *ME*, FROM BABES TO WOMANHOOD.
"SINCE THE ORIGINAL ABIGAIL WAS...DISAPPOINTING, I FIGURED I'D TRY AGAIN, SEED MORE THAN *ONE* THIS TIME AROUND...
UNH!
A WHOLE *FLOCK* OF THEM! OF OURSE, WANTING HAT'S BEST FOR THESE LITTLE BIGAILS, I TRIED CORRECT WHAT WENT WRONG THE FIRST TIME....
CRRRA
"SO I MADE SURE TO REMOVE NEARLY *ALL* OF THAT PESKY BRAIN OF HERS!"
ND YOU, BAKER... DOESN'T YOUR EAUTIFUL LITTLE GIRL JUST MAKE OU THE PROUDEST PARENT IN THE WORLD?"
PATHETIC! WEAK! SSSSSAD LITTLE REDTHING!
YOU ARE *NOT* MY MAXINE! WHERE IS SHE?! WHAT HAVE YOU DONE TO HER!?

OH IT'SSSS MEEE, DADDY...ALL GROWN UP. EVOLVE OR DIE, REMEMBER? YOU TAUGHT ME THAT.
ARRGH!
AND AS FOR THE PRECIOUS LITTLE RED QUEEN... WELL THAT'S HER ALL RIGHT, BAKER. THE REAL THING.
AND DENY IT AS YOU MIGHT, YOU SEE THAT. DON'T YOU? A FATHER ALWAYS KNOWS HIS BABY GIRL.
YOU SHOULD KNOW THAT SHE CAME OVER TO OUR SIDE FREELY, DIDN'T YOU, DEAR?
OH YESSSSSSS UNCLE ANTON... SSSSSO FREELY.
AND YOU, HOLLAND...HASN'T OUR ABBY FINALLY COME IN TO HER OWN?
HOLLAND, BAKER!
I'LL KILL YOU, ARCANE! DO YOU HEAR ME?!
WE'RE BEING OVERWHELMED! YOU HAVE TO FIGHT!

HA HA! YOU'VE NOTHING LEFT TO FIGHT FOR, BUDDY BAKER...
WE'VE TAKEN YOUR LITTLE WING. SSSSSHE IS A HUNTER OF THE THREE...SSSSHE IS OURS FOREVER. BODY AND SSSOUL.
THEY ARE WHY YOU SENSED ABIGAIL ALIVE IN THIS WORLD! THEY WERE THE BEACON YOU FOLLOWED ALL THIS WAY!
I WON'T LET YOU HAVE HER. NOT ANYMORE.
YOU MAY HAVE TAKEN HER BODY...TWISTED AND PERVERTED IT...
BUT YOU CAN'T HAVE MY BABY GIRL!

SHE'S TOO GOOD FOR YOU. TOO GOOD FOR THIS WORLD!
SHLUNK
YEEAARRG
DADDYYYY...
BAKER! GET UP, THIS ISN'T OVER!!
I-I'M DONE. THERE'S NO POINT.
NO POINT!?
THIS WORLD NEEDS YOU! THE SURVIVORS NEED YOU. THE HUMAN RACE IS ON THE VERGE OF EXTINCTION. YOU BETTER DAMNED WELL WAKE THE HELL UP!

STEEL! THE BAT-BOT, CAN YOU ACCESS IT AND--
BAKER! THERE'S TOO MANY OF THEM! WE NEED TO GET THE BAT-BOT UP INTO THE ATMOSPHERE AND RELEASE THE FORMULA! NOW!
ALREADY ON IT-- BUT I NEED TO GET CLOSER!
FEAR NOT, STEEL. BEAST BOY AND I SHALL CLEAR A PATH THROUGH THESE UNHOLY VERMIN!
OH, YES... SCURRY, LITTLE BUGS. MAKE YOUR PLANS!
DON'T YOU UNDERSTAND? YOU CANNOT STOP THIS! THE ROT OF EVERYTHING IS INEVITABLE!
WOULD SOMEONE PLEASE SHUT THAT OLD BASTARD UP?
WE'VE GOT THE HARPIES! GO, GO!!
SKLTCH
COME ON, GIRL...
...COME ON!
RRMMMMBBL
FWOOOOSH

IT'S WORKING! IT'S--
IT'S OVER.
ALL OF IT, YOUR LITTLE QUEST... IT ENDS HERE AND NOW...
...AS SOON AS I SEND YOUR DEAR ROBOT CRASHING BACK DOWN TO EARTH.
NO!

HE'S DESTROYING IT-- RIPPING OUT THE CONTROLS!
IT NEEDS TO IGNITE IN THE ATMOSPHERE! IF IT BLOWS TOO SOON, IT'S USELESS!
BAKER, ARE YOU ALL RIGHT?
NO. BUT I'M NOT LETTING THAT EVIL BASTARD HURT ANYONE ELSE!
KZZZT
LOOK AT YOU, ALWAYS TRYING--
--AND ALWAYS, ALWAYS TOO LATE!
SHUT THE HELL UP!
HA HA HA HA

I'VE GOT ARCANE!
OH, THE LITTLE ANIMAL MAN HAS GOT ME? HA!
JUST GET THIS THING UP INTO THE ATMOSPHERE!
I'M-- UNGH--I'M TRYING!
COME ON ALEC!
USE EVERYTHING YOU'VE GOT LEFT, EVERY OUNCE OF LIFE...
IT'S WHAT THE GREEN DOES-- FIGHT UP FROM THE GROUND!
UP THROUGH THE DARK! COME ON, YOU BASTARD CLIMB! CLIMB TOWARDS THE LIGHT!

ARRRGH!!
THIS DANCE IS ENDLESS! DON'T YOU SEE THAT?
UNGH!
BUT PLEASE... DO KEEP TRYING! IT'S WHAT MAKES THIS SO MUCH FUN. YOUR BELIEF, YOUR HOPE!
BAKER!
YOUR BELIEF THAT BECOMING THIS GREEN MONSTER--
--WOULD MATTER.
THAT YOU MIGHT AFFECT THINGS...

I'VE GOT YOU!
I-I GOTTA GET BACK UP THERE...BUT I'M SPENT. THE RED IS SO WEAK TO BEGIN WITH...
WHAT IF...
WHAT?
WHAT IF I GIVE HIM MY POWER...LET HIM CHANNEL THE RED THROUGH ME?
BUT YOU'D BE HELPLESS DOWN HERE!
THERE IS NO TIME FOR DEBATE!
ARCANE IS TEARING SWAMP THING APART UP THERE!
I WILL HOLD THESE CREATURES AT BAY! HURRY!
GAR... ARE YOU SURE?
YOU'RE THE BEST THERE IS WITH THESE POWERS. JUST DO IT.
I-I THINK IT'S WORKING. BUT BEAST BOY, HE'S--
DON'T STOP!

KEEP TRYING, DR. HOLLAND! BUT I'LL NEVER LET YOU REACH--
GO ALEC! DO IT! QUICKLY!
I'LL MAKE YOU SUFFER ENDLESSLY FOR THIS, BAKER! ENDLESSLY!
MAYBE, ANTON! BUT NOT TODAY! TODAY, YOU AND I ARE GOING TO SIT BACK--

"--AND WATCH THE *RAIN* FALL."

BEEP
IGNITION

ALEC.
BAKER... DID I--
YES, ALEC--
"--I THINK IT WORKED!
"THE GREEN RAIN, IT'S BURNING THROUGH THE ROT. WAKING THE WORLD UP."
DAMN YOU, HOLLAND! THIS IS NOT OVER--
--I'LL JUST MAKE YOU HURT MORE NEXT TIME!
ARCANE'S GETTING TO COVER--
WE... SAW HIM...

ALEC, YOU NEED TO STOP. YOUR LIFE FORCE, YOUR HUMAN BODY...I CAN FEEL IT DY--
THERE'S NO TIME!
OH, MY BRAVE, BOLD KNIGHTS. MY WARRIORS TRUE.
YOU NEVER DISAPPOINT, DO YOU? GATHERING YOUR ARMIES. MARCHING ON MY KINGDOM, HEARTS FULL OF COURAGE.
DON'T YOU SEE? IT DOESN'T MATTER? NONE OF IT? I *OWN* DEATH. AND DEATH IS TIMELESS. I CAN JUST GO BACK AND DO IT AGAIN AND AGAIN UNTIL I WIN!
DON'T LET HIM JUMP, ALEC--
ENDLESS DEATH! THE ROT HAS WON!
I CAN'T *HOLD* HIM!
NO!

TOO LATE...
WE'RE TOO LATE.
DAMN IT! IT WAS ALL FOR NOTHING!
DEATH AND LIFE ARE ONE, ALEC HOLLAND.
IF NOTHING ELSE, YOU SHOULD HAVE LEARNED THAT BY NOW.
LIFE IS THE GATEWAY TO DEATH. AND DEATH, IN ALL LIFE, STILL ECHOES.
AND THOSE ECHOES RESONATE HERE IN THE BOWELS OF THE ROT...IN US... THE PARLIAMENT OF DECAY!

BAKER...
I'VE GOT YOUR BACK, BIG MAN.
WE ARE NOT YOUR ENEMY, BUDDY BAKER.
IT IS ANTON ARCANE'S HEART THAT IS BLACK, NOT THE ROT'S.
AND THE STRONGER HE GETS, THE WEAKER WE, THE FORMER AVATARS OF DECAY, GROW.
BUT WE HAVE ENOUGH POWER LEFT TO OPEN A RIFT IN HIS WAKE.
I—I DON'T UNDERSTAND. WHY ARE YOU HELPING US? ARCANE IS YOUR AVATAR!
WE WERE FOOLS TO TRUST ARCANE. THIS WORLD HE HAS MADE IN OUR NAME, IT'S AN ABOMINATION TO THE FORCES OF BOTH LIFE AND DEATH. IT IS CRUMBLING, BUT HE HAS ESCAPED INTO THE TIMELESS VOID OF DEATH.
HE WILL JUST REMAKE IT AGAIN AND AGAIN UNTIL HIS NIGHTMARE VISION IS COMPLETE.

HE HAS TWISTED THE NATURAL ORDER OF THE BALANCE. TAKEN CONTROL OF THE ROT AND PERVERTED IT INTO A THING OF EVIL THAT IT WAS NEVER MEANT TO BE.
IF BALANCE IS NOT RESTORED, EVERYTHING WILL BE LOST. WE ONLY HAVE THE POWER TO SEND YOU BACK ONCE...IF YOU FAIL, WE WILL NOT BE ABLE TO HELP YOU AGAIN.
ALEC, WHAT IF IT'S A TRICK? YOU AND I HAVE BOTH BEEN DECEIVED BY OUR OWN ELEMENTS IN THE PAST... WHO KNOWS IF THIS WILL ONLY MAKE THINGS WORSE AND--
I KNOW. I HAVE THE SAME FEARS, BUT IF THERE'S EVEN A CHANCE WE CAN GO BACK, SAVE ABBY AND YOUR FAMILY, PREVENT THIS FROM HAPPENING...
I KNOW. WE HAVE TO TRY.
WHATEVER IT TAKES, BUDDY, WE HAVE TO STOP ARCANE.
WHATEVER IT TAKES.

JEFF LEMIRE
writer

STEVE PUGH
artist

JAE LEE
cover artist

HURRY, BUDDY BAKER... ALEC HOLLAND...THIS WORLD, THIS HOUSE OF CARDS THAT ARCANE MADE, IT'S CRUMBLING. BUT HE HAS ESCAPED INTO THE TIMELESS VOID OF DEATH, AND WILL JUST REMAKE HIS ROTWORLD AGAIN AND AGAIN UNTIL HIS NIGHTMARE VISION IS COMPLETE.
I--I DON'T UNDERSTAND. WHY ARE YOU HELPING US? ANTON ARCANE IS YOUR AVATAR!
HE HAS TWISTED THE NATURAL ORDER OF THE BALANCE BETWEEN THE RED, THE ROT AND THE GREEN. TAKEN CONTROL OF THE ROT FROM US AND PERVERTED IT INTO A THING OF EVIL.
IF BALANCE IS NOT RESTORED, EVERYTHING WILL BE LOST. WE ONLY HAVE THE POWER TO SEND YOU BACK ONCE...IF YOU FAIL, WE WILL NOT BE ABLE TO HELP YOU AGAIN.
WE HAVE NO CHOICE, BUDDY. WE MAY HAVE SAVED THIS WORLD, BUT FOR WHAT? EVERYONE WE KNOW, EVERYONE WE LOVE IS GONE.
IF THERE IS EVEN A CHANCE WE CAN GO BACK, SAVE ABBY AND YOUR FAMILY, PREVENT THIS FROM HAPPENING...
I KNOW. WE HAVE TO TRY.
WHATEVER IT TAKES, BUDDY, WE HAVE TO STOP ARCANE.
WHATEVER IT TAKES.

THE INSTANT WE OBEY THE PARLIAMENT OF DECAY, AND ENTER THE ROT, SWAMP THING AND I ARE SEPARATED... PULLED APART.
MY BOWELS TWIST AND I FEEL A SLOSH IN MY GUT AND I CAN'T GET MY BEARINGS.
I'VE JOURNEYED TO THE HEART OF THE RED ITSELF. I'VE CHANNELED THE ABILITIES OF LIONS, LIZARDS, MICROSCOPIC ORGANISMS...BONDED WITH THEM IN THE MORPHOGENETIC FIELD, THE LIFEWEB THAT CONNECTS ALL ANIMAL LIFE.
BUT THIS...THIS IS THE WEIRDEST, MOST UNSETTLING SENSATION I'VE EVER HAD...I'M FALLING, BUT I'M NOT FALLING DOWN ANYMORE, I'M FALLING UP.
AND IT'S NOT JUST THROUGH SOME PORTAL...SOME LOOP IN TIME. THIS IS SOMETHING DIFFERENT; SOMETHING SO IMMENSE I ALMOST GO MAD TRYING TO PERCEIVE IT.
I'M SAILING THROUGH ENDLESS EONS OF DEATH ITSELF...WALLS MADE OF THE DEAD A BILLION SOULS DEEP.
AND ALL AROUND ME THEY CALL OUT...THEIR VOICES IN AGONY. ALL THE LOST SOULS CONVERTED TO THE ROT BY ARCANE...THEIR FLESH USED TO POPULATE HIS HORRIBLE WORLD.

SOME I RECOGNIZE, FAMILIAR HEROES WHO I WAS FORCED TO FACE IN BATTLE. THEY NEED MY HELP. THEY NEED TO BE FREE.
BUT I DON'T HEAR THEM...MY CHILDREN, MAXINE AND CLIFF. MY WIFE...MY ELLEN...
AND WHILE IT MAY BE SELFISH, THEY ARE ALL I CARE ABOUT NOW. THE THOUGHT OF THEM IS ALL THAT KEEPS ME FROM BEING LOST AMONGST THE DAMNED.
SO I LET THOSE THOUGHTS PULL ME UP AND OUT OF THIS TERRIBLE PLACE. ELLEN'S BREATH AGAINST MY NECK. MAXINE'S RED HAIR IN MY HANDS...CLIFF'S SMILE...

LOUISIANA. NOW.
AND THEN IT ENDS.
CRACK
AND I'M BACK.
ARRGH!
ROTWORLD:
ROTWORLD: THE RED KINGDOM epilogue

SO DISORIENTED...FORGOT TO PROTECT MYSELF WHEN I FELL. DISLOCATED SHOULDER...BONE PUSHED RIGHT THROUGH MY FOREARM.
BUT I SHOULD HEAL QUICKLY. FOR THE FIRST TIME SINCE I WENT THROUGH THAT PORTAL INTO ARCANE'S WORLD, I CAN FEEL THE FULL POWER OF THE RED PUMPING THROUGH MY BLOOD.
--THE HELL?
SPLORT
MRRFF MMRR
MRR OFF OF ME!
UNGH!
SPLAT
I DON'T WAIT FOR IT TO COME BACK AT ME. I DON'T NEED TO. THE RV IS EMPTY, ANYWAY. I KNOW THEY AREN'T HERE...NOT ANYMORE.
BUT I HAVE THEIR TRAIL...IT'S FAINT, BURIED UNDER THE DEATH AND DECAY... A TRAIL TO MAXINE AND SOCKS!

WHEN CLIFF WAS A LITTLE BOY--ONLY FOUR OR FIVE--HE HAD THIS BOOK THAT SHOWED HIM HOW TO MAKE DIFFERENT ANIMALS USING FINGER PAINTS AND HIS HANDPRINTS.
HE LOVED THAT BOOK SO MUCH. EVERY NIGHT WE'D SIT AT THE DINING ROOM TABLE AND PICK WHICH ANIMAL HE WANTED TO MAKE NEXT. ROOSTERS. DOGS. SEALS.
ELLEN KEPT THEM ALL, STRUNG THEM UP ON A CLOTHESLINE ACROSS THE LIVING ROOM.
IT'S FUNNY, BUT EVEN TODAY, WHENEVER I ACCESS MY POWERS AND CONNECT WITH DIFFERENT ANIMALS, I ALWAYS THINK OF CLIFF AND THAT BOOK. THE WAY HE'D FLIP THE PAGES AND POINT TO ANOTHER ONE.
NO MATTER HOW BAD THINGS GET, I ALWAYS GO BACK TO THAT. I IMAGINE HIS LITTLE HAND SWIRLING AROUND IN THE PAINT. I REMEMBER THE LOOK ON HIS FACE. SO HAPPY.

THE PARLIAMENT OF DECAY'S GAMBIT WORKED. MY FAMILY IS IN HERE. I CAN SENSE THEM...ALL OF THEM. AND THEY'RE STILL ALIVE!
BUT THEY'RE NOT ALONE.
YESSSS... COME TO USSSS, CHILD...COME TO THE ROT. A SSSIMPLE TRADE. YOUR LIFE FOR YOUR FAMILY...
DON'T BE SSSSCARED, LITTLE ONE... PUTREFACTION IS SSSSO BEAUTIFUL.
M-MOM?
--UNGH...
MAXINE, NO!
OH, CLIFF! THANK GOD YOU'RE ALL RIGHT!

MAXINE! WHAT ARE YOU DOING!?
IT'S THE ONLY WAY, MOMMY...
NO!
IT ISSSS ALREADY DONE...
THWUNK
MAXINE!
DADDY!
SSSSSSS

BUDDY! OU HAVE TO TOP THEM... EY'RE TAKING MAXINE.
THESE MONSTERS AREN'T TAKING *ANYONE.*
IMPOSSSSSIBLE! ARCANE HAD YOU AND THE SWAMP THING TRAPPED....THIS ISSSS *OUR* WORLD NOW. HE PROMISSSSED!
ARRGH!
YOU BE QUIET!

I'LL RIP YOU APART, BAKER... MAKE YOU SSSSCREAM FOR MERCY!
THERE IS NOTHING... NOTHING THAT IS GOING TO TAKE ME AWAY FROM MY FAMILY AGAIN. NOT ARCANE...NOT YOU.
SMASH!
SSSSSSS
SO JUST DIE ALREADY!
YOU THINK YOUR STUPID HUSBAND CAN STOP US?
HUURK
MOM!
THWACK
YOU ARE A BAD, BAD BOY, WILLIAM ARCANE!

STAY BACK, LITTLE WING...
I'M GONNA KILL THAT LITTLE BRAT!
SSSSSSSSILENCE, LITTLE ARCANE! YOU HAVE SSSSERVED YOUR PATHETIC PURPOSSSSE!
ARCANE IS MY UNCLE! I AM HIS BLOOD! YOU HAVE TO DO WHAT I SAY! HE PROMISED ME THE SEA!
ARCANE HAS FORSSSAKEN USSSSS!
SWAP
UNGH!
OH MY GOD!
HE--HE WAS JUST A KID!

WHATEVER HE DID, HE WAS STILL A LITTLE BOY!
YOUR SSSELF-RIGHTEOUSNESSS IS HILARIOUS, BUDDY BAKER! HE WASSSSS THE PRINCE OF EVIL.
HOLD STILL, SOCKS! I'M GONNA TAKE THE BAD STUFF OUT OF YOU.
THAT-- THAT IS MUCH BETTER, THANK YOU, CHILD.
LISTEN TO ME, MAXINE...YOUR FATHER CANNOT STOP THEM ON HIS OWN.
HE NEEDS YOU!
NO! BUDDY KNOWS WHAT HE'S DOING!
MAXINE, YOU ARE NOT TO DO ANYTHING! STAY AWAY!
BUT MOMMMYY...
NO!
HOLD ON, DAD! I'M COMING!

CLIFF! NO!
BUT I JUST WANT TO HELP DAD!
WHUMP
DO NOT COME ANY CLOSER, CLIFF!

NO!
UNGH GET BACK!
SPLORK!

DO YOU NOT SEE, ELLEN BAKER? THEY JUST KEEP COMING AND COMING. YOU CANNOT KILL THEM.

THEY HAVE CHASED YOUR FAMILY ACROSS THE COUNTRY. TERRORIZED YOU AND PUT YOUR CHILDREN IN JEOPARDY AGAIN AND AGAIN.
IF WE--IF MAXINE DOES NOT END THIS ONCE AND FOR ALL, THEY WILL NEVER STOP!

WHAT YOU DON'T SEEM TO UNDERSTAND IS THAT SHE IS ONLY A LITTLE GIRL! MY LITTLE GIRL!

NO, ELLEN BAKER. SHE IS SO MUCH MORE. AND SHE BELONGS TO EVERYONE.
SHE IS THE ALL-MOTHER. SHE IS THE GIVER OF LIFE. SHE IS OUR SALVATION.

THEY ARE TERRIFIED OF HER. THEY ALWAYS HAVE BEEN. THAT'S WHY THEY HAD TO TRICK HER INTO GIVING HERSELF OVER WILLINGLY.

WHAT DO I DO, SOCKS? JUST TELL ME.
MAXINE, YOU JUST PULLED THE ROT FROM MY BONES, HEALED ME...DO YOU KNOW HOW YOU DID THAT?
I JUST PULLED IT OUT AND MADE ALL THE GOOD STUFF GROW BACK. I DON'T KNOW HOW I DID IT. I JUST DID.
YES! YOU PULLED THE BAD STUFF, THE ROT, OUT. YOU NEED TO DO THAT AGAIN...TO THEM, THE HUNTERS.
YOU SEE, CHILD, WE MAY NOT BE ABLE TO KILL THE HUNTERS, BUT YOU CAN CHANGE THEM.
FOR WHAT IS LIFE IF NOT A CYCLE? BIRTH, DEATH, DECAY AND REBIRTH. DO YOU UNDERSTAND?
I--I THINK SO. LIKE WHEN I GREW MYSELF AGAIN OUT OF THAT FOX.
YES! PRECISELY!
SSSSSSO... THE LITTLE FLESHLING WANTSSSS TO PLAY?
NO, MAXINE!
DON'T WORRY, DADDY... I'VE GOT THIS.
I REALLY DO WISH I HAD A COSTUME, THOUGH.

SSSSSSSSTOP! GET OUT!
SHE INVADESSS!
OH! I SEE YOU NOW!
I CAN SEE WHAT YOU REALLY ARE... WHO YOU USED TO BE!
YOU'RE NOT REALLY SCARY AT ALL!
LEASSSE--
IT'S OKAY. DON'T BE SAD...I THINK I CAN HELP YOU.
UNGH SO MUCH ROTTEN STUFF IN YOU NOW. HURTS SO BAD.
LITTLE WING?
IT'S UNGH IT'S OKAY, DADDY... I'M FINDING THEM IN THERE...GROWING THEM AGAIN.
OH, JESUS!
SEE? IT'S JUST THEM. THE REAL THEM. LIKE THEY USED TO BE BEFORE THE BAD STUFF GOT THEM.

OH, GOD!
GASP
THANKS FOR HEALING MY ARM...I'VE GOT YOU, LITTLE WING.

MAXINE!
SHE'S OKAY. SHE JUST PASSED OUT. SHE'S FINE.
COME HERE, BABY.
WH-WHERE ARE WE?
WHAT HAPPENED? ARE YOU WITH *TAPROOT?* WH-WHERE'S *THE ASCENSION CHAMBER?*
TAPROOT? THE ASCENSION CHAMBER? I THOUGHT THE TOTEMS SAID THESE GUYS USED TO BE ANIMAL MEN... AVATARS WHO WERE CORRUPTED? WHAT ARE THEY TALKING ABOUT?
THEY WERE... I'VE NO IDEA WHAT TO MAKE OF THIS.
WELL, RIGHT NOW, I DON'T CARE. I'M JUST GLAD THIS IS OVER. IT IS SO GOOD TO SEE YOU, CLIFFY BOY!
YOU HAVE NO IDEA HOW MUCH I MISSED YOU.
OKAY, OKAY. WATCH THE BEAR HUG, DAD.
ELLEN. I'M SO SORRY... I WAS LOST, IN ANOTHER WORLD. THE ROT HAD WON. YOU WERE ALL GONE. IT WAS HORRIBLE.
I--I CAN'T--
ELLEN?

ELLEN, PLEASE. I DIDN'T MEAN FOR ANY OF THIS TO HAPPEN!
YOU NEVER MEAN FOR ANYTHING BAD TO HAPPEN, BUDDY. BUT IT DOES. AGAIN AND AGAIN.
ELLEN, PLEASE--
D-DAD!
WHA--?
DAD, LOOK OUT-- URK
CLIFF!
NO!
OH, GOD!

YOU CAN'T ESCAPE IT, BAKER. DEATH ALWAYS WINS...
THE ROT ALWAYS WINS.
CLIFF?!
HAK
OH MY BABY!
I-I SAVED YOU, DAD--
...HERO-- JUST LIKE YOU--
CLIFF?!

JEFF LEMIRE
writer

STEVE PUGH
artist

HOWARD PORTER
cover artist

SAN DIEGO.
HOTEL

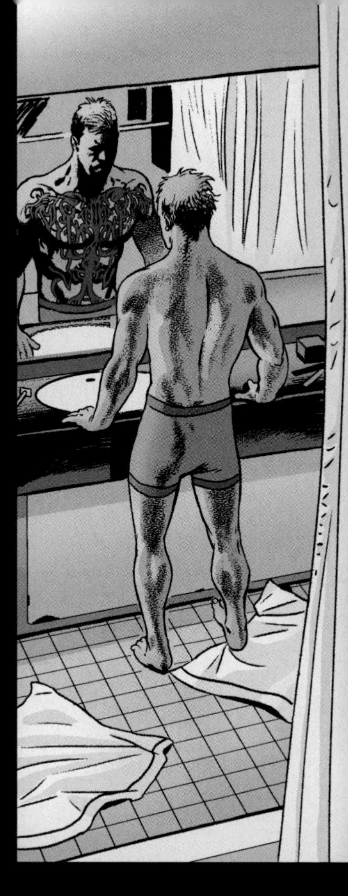

ELLEN?

ELLEN... IT'S TIME, DEAR.
I-I CAN'T.

OH, SWEETIE... I KNOW IT'S HARD. BUT YOU HAVE TO.
NO. I DON'T.
I DON'T *HAVE* TO DO *ANYTHING* ANYMORE.

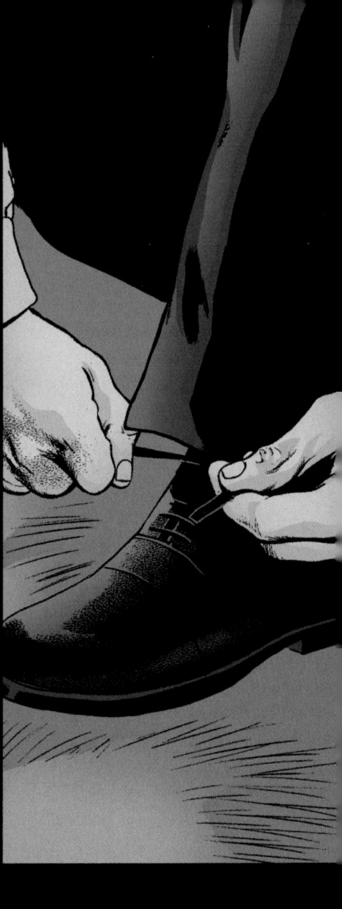

THIS IS--
THIS IS THE HARDEST THING YOU WILL *EVER* HAVE TO DO. I DON'T NEED TO TELL YOU THAT. BUT MAXINE IS DOWNSTAIRS AND SHE'S JUST AS SCARED AND SAD AS YOU ARE.

OH, HELL. MAYBE YOU'RE RIGHT. MAYBE IT DOESN'T MATTER. I JUST DON'T KNOW ANY-MORE.

I'LL BE DOWNSTAIRS WITH MAXINE. WE'RE GOING.
YOU'RE RIGHT. YOU DON'T *HAVE* TO COME. BUT YOU SHOULD. FOR CLIFF.

THE FUNERAL

--IT IS HARD EVEN TO FATHOM THE LOSS OF A CHILD. HOW CAN WE--ANY OF US--TRY TO TELL CLIFF'S FAMILY OR FRIENDS THAT WE UNDERSTAND... THAT WE'RE SORRY?--
UNLESS WE'VE EXPERIENCED SUCH AN INCREDIBLE LOSS OURSELVES, WE CAN'T EVEN BEGIN TO CONSOLE THEM.
THE ONLY COMFORT WE *CAN* OFFER IS THAT LOOKING AT HIS FAMILY HERE TODAY--WE CAN SEE HOW MUCH CLIFF WAS LOVED IN HIS SHORT BUT FULL LIFE.
WE MAY NOT UNDERSTAND WHAT BUDDY, ELLEN AND MAXINE ARE FEELING. BUT WE DO UNDERSTAND HOW PRECIOUS THE LIFE WE'VE BEEN GIVEN IS. AND WE CAN HOLD ONTO ONE ANOTHER NOW IN THIS TERRIBLE TIME.
CLIFFORD BUDDY BAKER
MAY 6, 20
-FEBRUARY 18, 2
BELOVED SON AND BROTHER
CLIFF WAS LOVED. AND HIS LOSS WILL NOT BE AN EASY THING TO OVERCOME. BUT REMEMBER, HE IS STILL HERE. WE CARRY HIM WITH US NOW. AND HE WILL GIVE US THE STRENGTH WE NEED TO CARRY ON.

ELLEN, PLEASE. WAIT.
MOMMY! STOP!

LOOK, ELLEN, WE NEED TO TALK. PLEASE.
THIS ISN'T THE TIME!
STAY OUT OF IT, MOM!
I JUST--NOT NOW, BUDDY. MAYBE IN A BIT, BUT...JUST NOT NOW.

BUT, ELLEN... THERE STILL MIGHT BE A CHANCE. IF WE JUST LET MAXINE TRY TO--
NO! DON'T YOU EVEN SAY IT! DON'T YOU DARE!

THAT IS OVER. NO MORE POWERS... NO MORE CRAZY STUFF! NO MORE! FROM NOW ON MAXINE IS--MAXINE IS NORMAL.
BUT SHE'S NOT NORMAL! NO MATTER HOW MUCH YOU WANT THAT.
I DIDN'T CHOOSE THIS. THE RED CHOSE US. AND IF SHE CAN STILL-- I DON'T KNOW--HELP CLIFF SOMEHOW-- FIND HIM--
SLAP!
HE'S DEAD, DAMMIT! DON'T YOU DARE TRY TO MAKE THAT A PART OF YOUR CRAZINESS, TOO.
JUST LET HIM GO. FOR GOD'S SAKE, JUST LET HIM REST.
I JUST CAN'T DO ANY OF IT ANYMORE.
...EVERY TIME I LOOK IN YOUR EYES I JUST SEE CLIFF.
ELLEN... WHAT ARE YOU SAYING?

IT'S OVER, BUDDY. I CAN'T BE WITH YOU ANYMORE.

BUDDY! HOW WAS THE FUNERAL? ARE YOU AND MRS. BAKER DIVORCING?

OH, COME ON...GIVE ME A BREAK.
BUDDY, IS THIS JUST A PUBLICITY STUNT LEADING INTO AWARDS SEASON?

YOU SCUMBAG! MY SON JUST DIED!

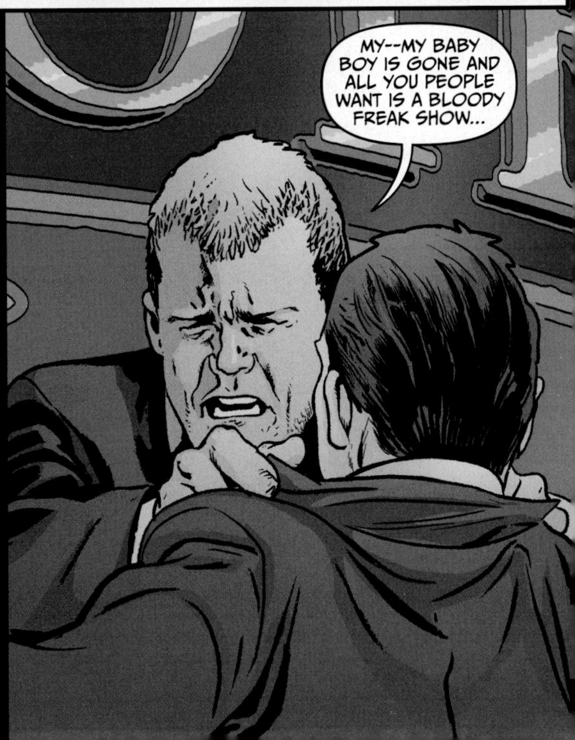
MY--MY BABY BOY IS GONE AND ALL YOU PEOPLE WANT IS A BLOODY FREAK SHOW...

WELL, HERE'S YOUR DAMN FREAK SHOW!
ANY OF YOU GO ANYWHERE NEAR MY FAMILY, AND I'LL KILL YOU.

≥PSST≤ IT'S OKAY... YOU CAN COME OUT NOW.
≥MREEOOE≤ LL OF THIS HIDING MOST UNDIGNIFIED. ERHAPS IF I SPOKE TO YOUR MOTHER--
NO! ARE YOU NUTS? IF MOMMY KNEW YOU WERE STILL HERE, SHE'D SKIN YOU! AND ME!
MOMMY DOESN'T WANT NOTHING TO DO WITH THE RED NO MORE. MAYBE SHE'S RIGHT. BUT I KEEP THINKING MAYBE I CAN STILL HELP CLIFFY.
I-I DON'T FEEL LIKE HE'S REALLY GONE YET.
MAYBE THAT'S WHY I'M NOT TOO SAD. MAYBE HE'S NOT REALLY DEAD YET.
HE IS DEAD, CHILD.
UNDERSTANDING THAT, ACCEPTING IT, IS THE FIRST STEP...

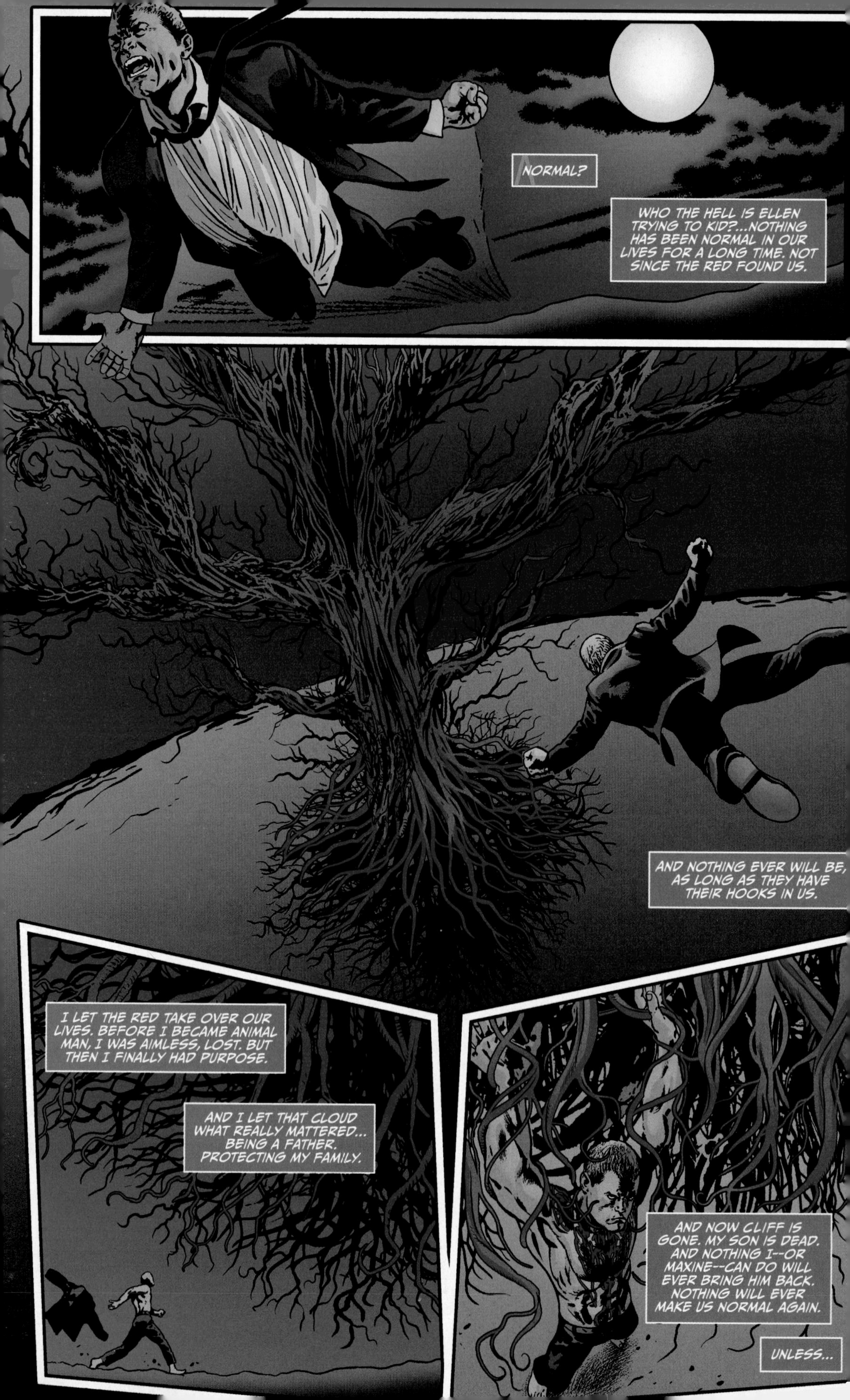
NORMAL?
WHO THE HELL IS ELLEN TRYING TO KID?...NOTHING HAS BEEN NORMAL IN OUR LIVES FOR A LONG TIME. NOT SINCE THE RED FOUND US.
AND NOTHING EVER WILL BE, AS LONG AS THEY HAVE THEIR HOOKS IN US.
I LET THE RED TAKE OVER OUR LIVES. BEFORE I BECAME ANIMAL MAN, I WAS AIMLESS, LOST. BUT THEN I FINALLY HAD PURPOSE.
AND I LET THAT CLOUD WHAT REALLY MATTERED... BEING A FATHER. PROTECTING MY FAMILY.
AND NOW CLIFF IS GONE. MY SON IS DEAD. AND NOTHING I--OR MAXINE--CAN DO WILL EVER BRING HIM BACK. NOTHING WILL EVER MAKE US NORMAL AGAIN.
UNLESS...

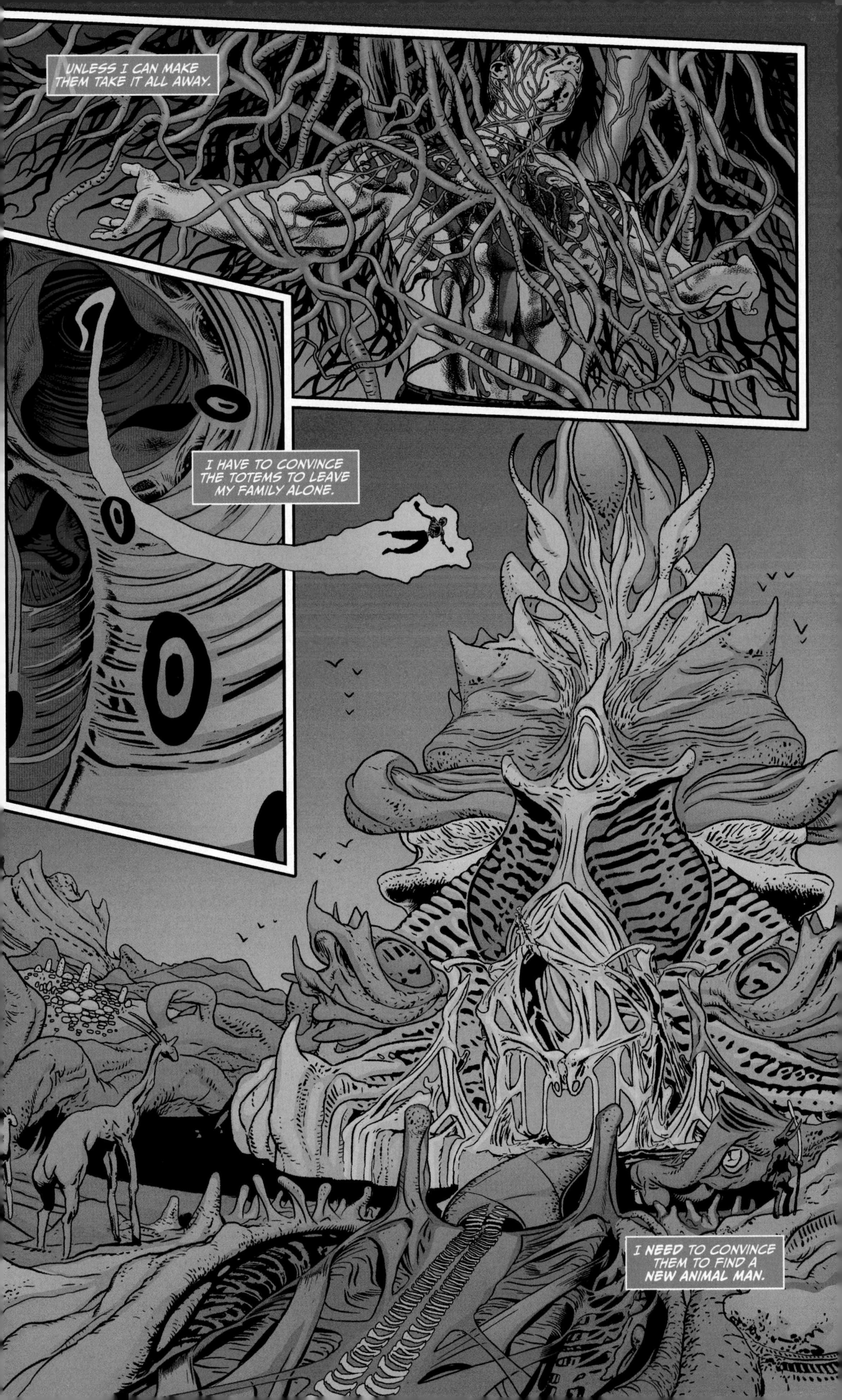
UNLESS I CAN MAKE THEM TAKE IT ALL AWAY.
I HAVE TO CONVINCE THE TOTEMS TO LEAVE MY FAMILY ALONE.
I NEED TO CONVINCE THEM TO FIND A NEW ANIMAL MAN.

LORD BAKER! WE ARE HONORED BY YOUR PRESENCE, SIR. I WAS NOT AWARE OF--*UM*--YOUR IMPENDING ARRIVAL.
SAVE IT. JUST OPEN THE DOOR.
SIR...THE *AHEM* TOTEMS ARE NOT TAKING VISITORS AT THIS TIME. AS I'M SURE YOU'RE AWARE, THE RED AND THE GREEN ARE IN FLUX IN THE WAKE OF THE ROT'S DEFEAT, AND THEY--
OPEN THIS DOOR. ***NOW.***
THAT SURE AS HECK AIN'T A GOOD IDEA YOU GOT BOUNCIN' AROUND IN THAT BLONDIE MAN NOGGIN OF YOURS, BUTTER BAKER!
OH? AND WHY THE HELL NOT, SHEPHERD?
'CAUSE YOU GOT YERSELF A HEAD FULLA STEA AND A BELLY FULLA AND RIGHTLY SO...I DON'T SUGGEST CARRY IT IN THER WITH YOU.
THE TOTEMS ARE NOT IN A...WELL LET'S JUST SAY THE LADIES AND FELLE AIN'T IN MUCH OF MOOD FOR TALKIN JUS' NOW.
THEY AREN'T IN THE MOOD? WELL, TOO DAMN BAD!

I'M NOT IN MUCH OF A MOOD EITHER!
>SIGH< WELL, DON'T SAY I DIDN'T WARN YA, BLONDIE MAN.
KA-THOOOOM
BUDDY BAKER! WHAT IS THE MEANING OF THIS INSOLENCE!
YOU CANNOT JUST STORM IN HERE LIKE THIS! THERE ARE RULES! EVEN FOR YOU!
YOU KNOW WHERE YOU CAN STICK YOUR DAMN RULES!
IT'S OVER. I'M DONE. I DON'T WANT TO BE ANIMAL MAN ANYMORE. AND MAXINE IS NOT YOUR DAMNED AVATAR. *IT'S ALL OVER!*

BAKER, WE ARE VERY SORRY ABOUT THE LOSS OF YOUR CHILD. LOSS IN WAR IS INEVITABLE. BUT HIS SACRIFICE ALLOWED MAXINE TO LIVE. IT ALLOWED FOR THE ROT TO FINALLY FALL BACK WHERE IT BELONGS.
AND YOU MUST UNDERSTAND, DEATH IS ONLY A GATEWAY. YOUR SON'S ESSENCE IS WITH US NOW. A PART OF THE LIFE WEB.
NO! I WILL NOT ACCEPT THAT. I WILL NOT ACCEPT THAT HE DIED FOR A GREATER GOOD. OR THAT IT IS OUR DESTINY TO SERVE YOU ANYMORE!
HE WAS JUST A CHILD. JUST A LITTLE BOY.
AND SHE'S JUST A LITTLE GIRL. IT'S OVER. YOU NEED TO CHOOSE A NEW ANIMAL MAN. A NEW AVATAR.
YOU NEED TO LEAVE US ALONE.

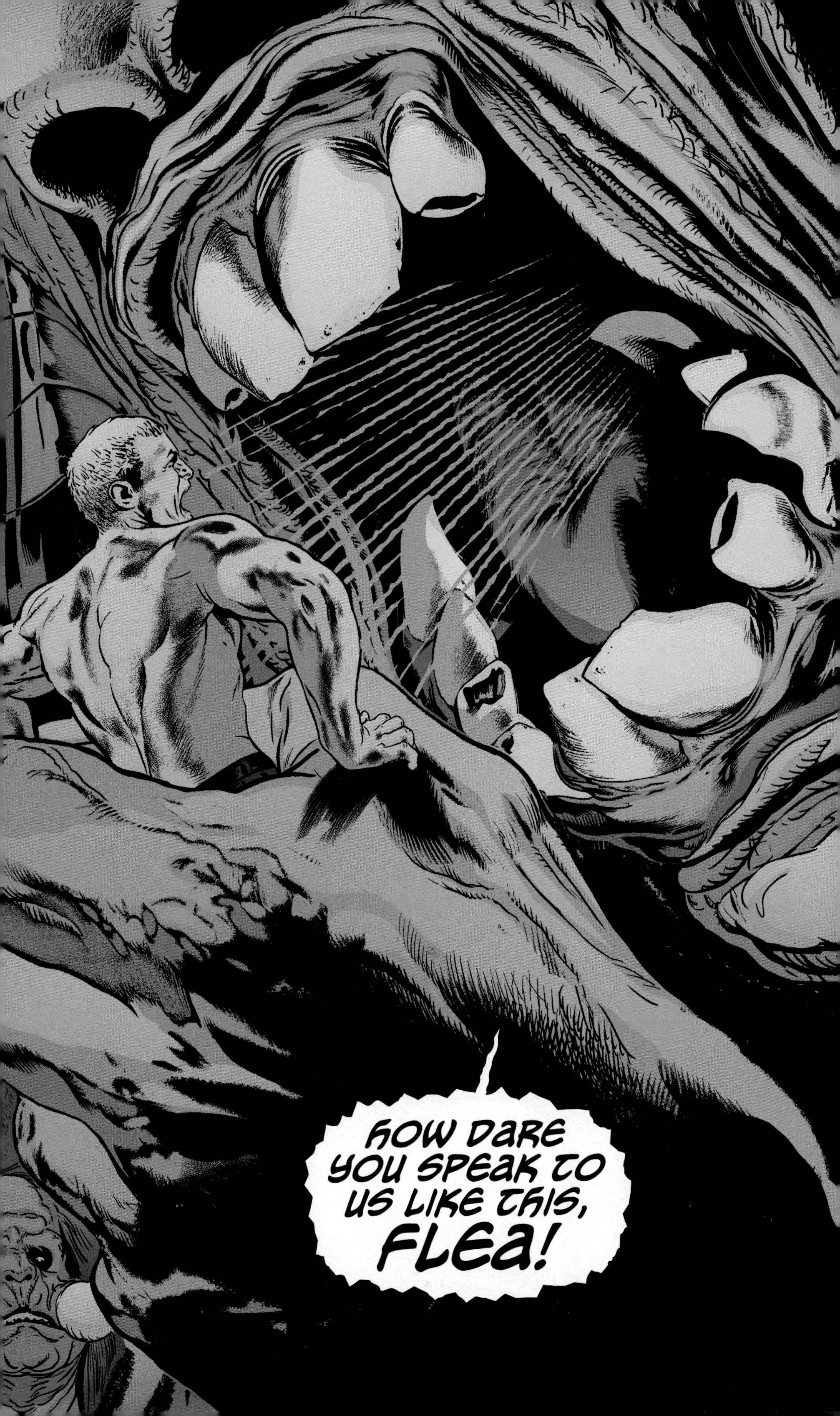
HOW DARE YOU SPEAK TO US LIKE THIS, FLEA!

TO BE OUR CHAMPION IS *AN HONOR!*
AND MAXINE IS *OURS!*
DO OUR BIDDING SHE IS READY.
BUT IF YOU DARE TRY TO IMPEDE US...TRY KEEP HER FROM WE WILL SIMPLY YOU AND YOUR OUT OF AND *TAKE* HER.
YOU WILL DO *OUR* BIDDING.
L-LET GO!
NO. WE WILL *NEVER* LET YOU GO. YOU ARE OURS. OUR PUPPET. OUR "ANIMAL MAN."
BE GONE, BUDDY BAKER... GO AND PLAY "SUPER HERO."
STOP!
AAARRRGH!
YOU HAVE LOST YOUR PRIVILEGES IN THE RED. YOU ARE NOT TO RETURN HERE UNLESS *WE* CALL ON *YOU!*

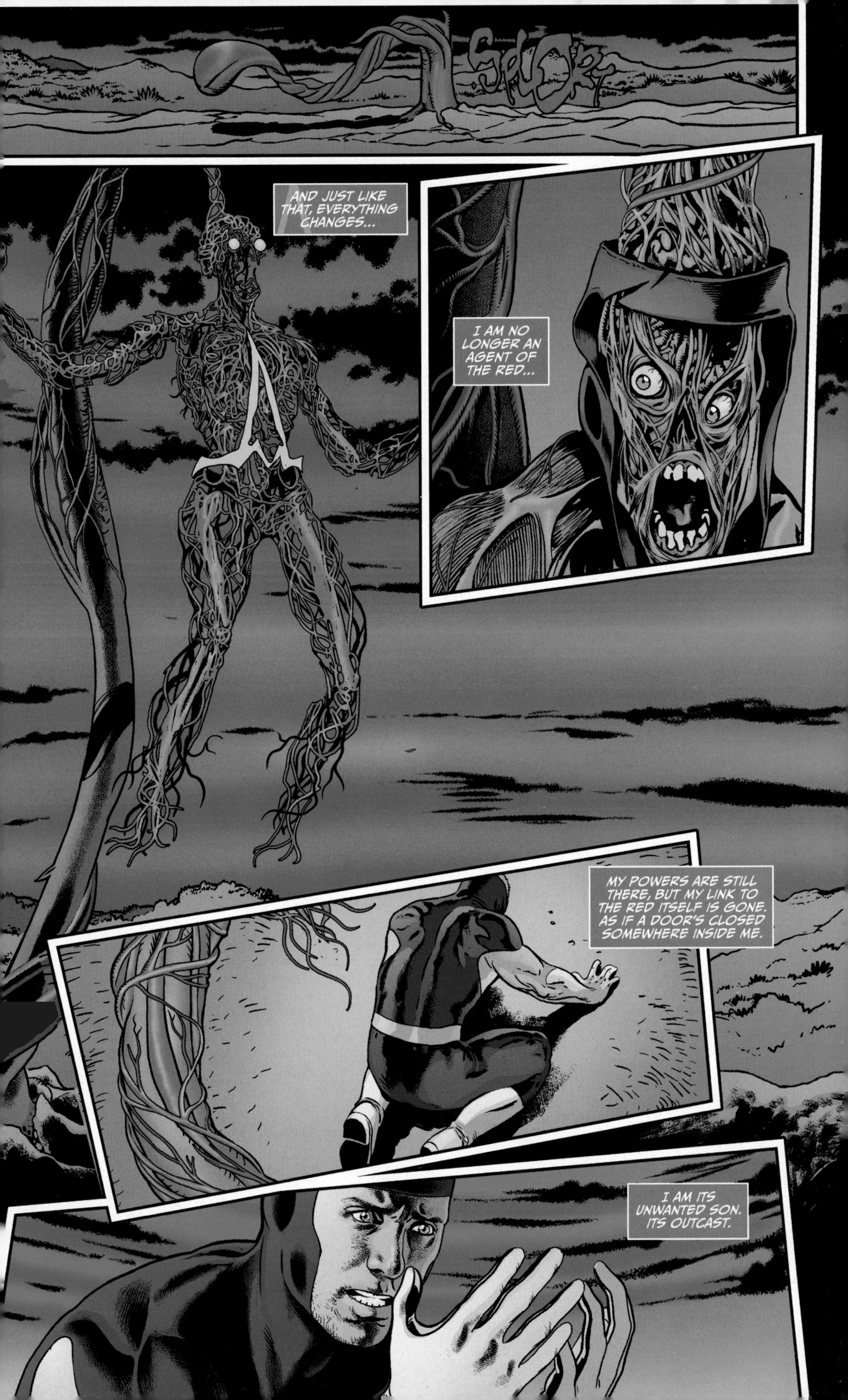
AND JUST LIKE THAT, EVERYTHING CHANGES...
I AM NO LONGER AN AGENT OF THE RED...
MY POWERS ARE STILL THERE, BUT MY LINK TO THE RED ITSELF IS GONE. AS IF A DOOR'S CLOSED SOMEWHERE INSIDE ME.
I AM ITS UNWANTED SON. ITS OUTCAST.

AND I'VE NEVER FELT SO ALONE IN MY LIFE.

Combined covers of ANIMAL MAN #12 and SWAMP THING #12

Combined covers of ANIMAL MAN #17 and SWAMP THING #17

FRANKENLANTERN
PHANTOM ARM
steP

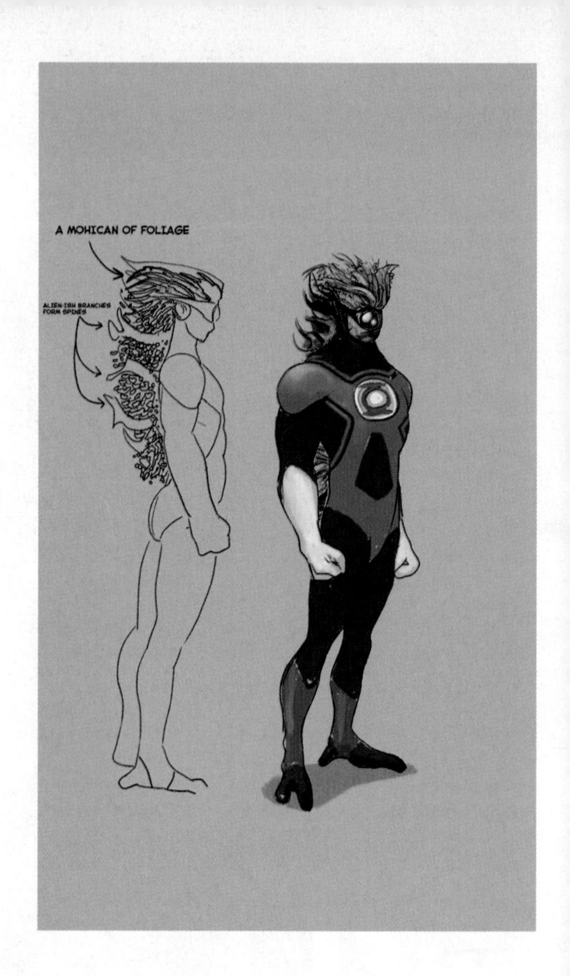
A MOHICAN OF FOLIAGE
ALIEN-ISH BRANCHES FORM SPINES

ROT QUEEN
MAXINE
steP

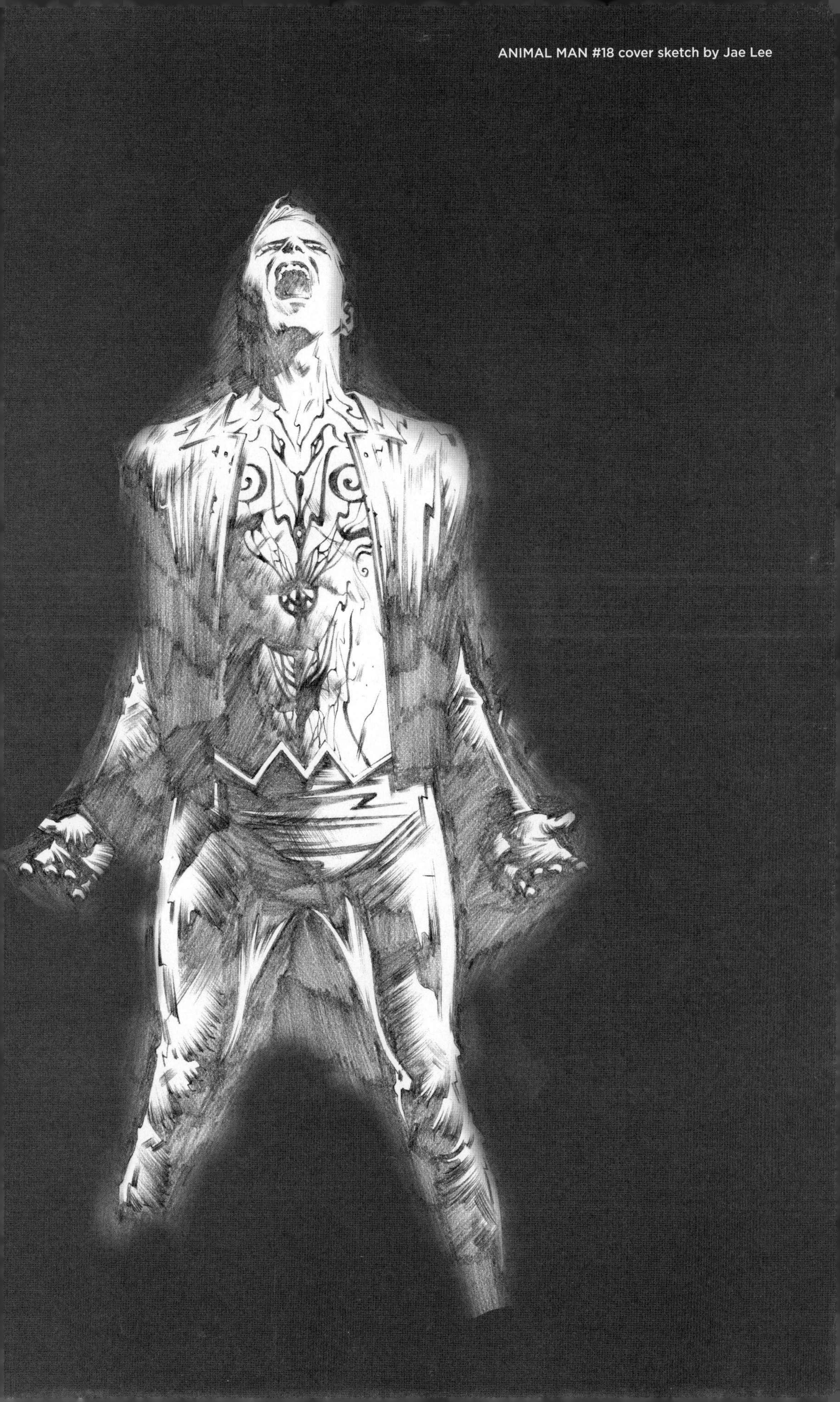

ANIMAL MAN #18 cover sketch by Jae Lee

ANIMAL MAN #19 Cover by HOWARD PORTER

LOVING MEMORY OF
CLIFFORD
BAKER